BRITISH RAILWAYS

PAST and PRESENT
Special

THE
PAIGNTON & DARTMOUTH
STEAM RAILWAY

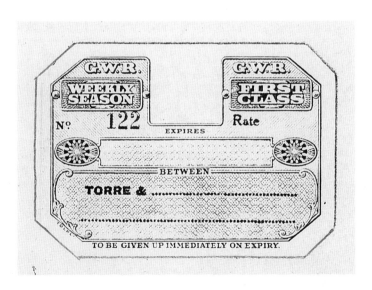

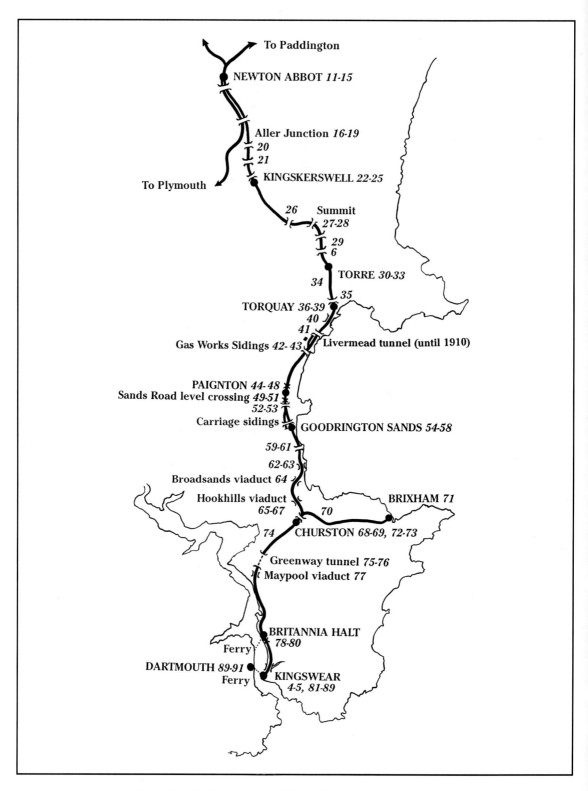

Map of the line from Newton Abbot to Kingswear and Dartmouth.
The numbers in italics refer to the page numbers where photographs of each location may be found.

BRITISH RAILWAYS

PAST and PRESENT
Special

THE
PAIGNTON & DARTMOUTH STEAM RAILWAY

A nostalgic trip down the line from Newton Abbot to Kingswear and Dartmouth

Peter W. Gray

"The English Rhine"
The centre for your holiday in the glorious
RIVER DART COUNTRY
is

DARTMOUTH
SOUTH DEVON

ILLUSTRATED GUIDE (P.O. 1/-) FROM DEPARTMENT H., GUILDHALL, DARTMOUTH

BR Holiday Guide, 1951

Past and Present

Past & Present Publishing Ltd

First published in April 1994

British Library Cataloguing in Publication Data

A catalogue record for this book is available from the British Library.

ISBN 1 85895 047 3

Past & Present Publishing Ltd
Unit 5
Home Farm Close
Church Street
Wadenhoe
Peterborough PE8 5TE
Tel/fax 0832 720440

Map on page 2 drawn by Christina Siviter

Printed and bound in Great Britain

A peaceful scene at Kingswear in the early years of this century (below), looking across Waterhead creek, with only a few terraces of houses looking down upon the level area which had to be reclaimed from the river so that Kingswear station and its then rather limited sidings could be constructed. The whitewashed cattle pens and early turntable stand out, while a '1016' Class 0-6-0 saddle tank and a '633' Class 0-6-0 side tank await their next turn of duty. *PWG Collection*

The sidings at Kingswear had been extended and then lifted before 2-6-2T No 4555 made the trial runs over the line on 30 July 1972, seen in the second photograph leaving Kingswear with two of the ex-GWR Special

Saloons, built for the Ocean Liner Expresses, and the Victorian Saloon next to the engine. *PWG*

The same view 20 years later (below right) shows the consider-able development that has taken place around Kingswear station, mostly in order to cope with the vast increase in leisure sailing and cruising that has been evident in the last ten years. For the Paignton & Dartmouth Steam Railway the final accolade was the arrival of the Royal Train on 10 April 1992 bring-ing HRH The Duke of Edinburgh on a visit to the Britannia Royal Naval College at Dartmouth. The empty Royal Train is here leaving Kingswear later than morning hauled by an immaculate Class '47', No 47834 *Fire Fly*. PWG

CONTENTS

'TITLED' TRAINS

THE "TORBAY EXPRESS"

As they leave Torre station behind, the 'Torbay Express' passengers will be settling down to enjoy a fast run to London and booking their seats in the Dining Car, as 'Castle' Class 4-6-0 No 5049 *Earl of Plymouth* accelerates confidently under Shiphay bridge on 28 July 1958. Some of the residents of the bed and breakfast establishments along Newton Road's 'Golden Mile' on the left appear to have been cultivating the level top of the embankment to their advantage, though they will have little time for this pursuit during the peak season.

Like the 'Torbay Express' of old, none of today's express trains stops at Torre, and the exhaust trail indicates the ease with which Class '47' No 47831 *Bolton Wanderer* is taking the seven-coach 08.39 Paignton to Glasgow train on 28 August 1993 past the ragged tangle of bushes that contrast so markedly with the tidy lineside of 1958. *Both PWG*

Advertisement from the BR Holiday Guide of 1951.

INTRODUCTION

Until the end of 1947, the line between Paignton and Kingswear, now the Paignton & Dartmouth Steam Railway, was part of the Great Western Railway's premier branch line from Newton Abbot down to the mouth of the river Dart at Kingswear, from whence the GWR's own steamship, *The Mew*, operated the passenger ferry service to Dartmouth. During the 1920s various structures along the line were strengthened, so that before the end of the decade the GWR's new 'King' Class locomotives, the heaviest engines on the line, were able to haul the 'Torbay Express' daily between London Paddington and Kingswear.

Since then the line has continued to be maintained in first class condition, and in recent years this has enabled visitors to the line to include a High Speed Train set, 'Deltic' Class diesel-electric locomotives, the Royal Train and in 1993 a return visit by arguably the most famous steam locomotive in the world, the ex-LNER 'Pacific' *Flying Scotsman*.

But it was not always thus. In the early days the South Devon Railway, which opened a single broad gauge line from Newton - it did not become Newton Abbot until 1877 - to Torquay in December 1848, terminated this at the then outskirts of the town, on the site of the present Torre station. The SDR had intended to work this line with the Atmospheric System of propulsion, which it was then using between Exeter and Newton, for which an Engine House had been constructed at the summit near Lawes (Lowes) bridge (see page 27), but the stationary engines ordered from Boulton & Watt were never installed, because three months prior to opening the SDR had decided to abandon the Atmospheric System in favour of locomotive haulage.

Consequently it was the hired GWR 2-4-0 saddle tank *Taurus* that hauled the first train into Torquay in December 1848. The initial service consisted only of six trains down and five up each day, later increased to seven, and an additional station at Kingskerswell was opened in July 1853.

Agitation for an extension of the line into the centre of Torquay, and even down to the harbour, arose more than once, but this was successfully opposed by the residents of Dartmouth, who felt that this would prejudice the eventual extension of the railway towards their town, as had been promised originally by the SDR. However, the parlous state of the SDR's finances meant that there was no prospect of it continuing the line beyond Torquay, and it was left to the independent Dartmouth & Torbay Railway, whose Act was passed in 1857, to continue the construction through Paignton and Churston to Kingswear. When complete, the line was to be worked by the SDR, and the first section to Paignton was opened in August 1859, at which time the land surrounding the station was open marshland, Paignton itself being then situated on rising ground a quarter of a mile inland.

In order to placate the agitators for a station in Torquay town centre, a new station was provided by the sea front, and the old Torquay station became Torre. But with the new station now regarded as the main station for Torquay, certain express trains omitted the Torre stop, an irritation for residents in the northern parts of the town that continues to this day.

Construction beyond Paignton continued across the marshland behind Goodrington sands, which gave some problems due to subsidence, and across Broadsands and Hookhills viaducts, both constructed of stone rather than the originally intended timber, to reach Brixham Road (later re-named Churston) in March 1861. Two years later the hotel outside the station was opened, during which time a horse omnibus plied to Greenway, connecting with a steamer service down the river to Dartmouth. Further progress was delayed by the need for more capital, and a proposal (fortunately rejected) to deviate the line down a zigzag gradient to terminate at

Greenway, with the intention of later bridging the River Dart. Further contracts were let in 1862, and work started on the Greenway tunnel and the three viaducts at Maypool, Longwood and Noss. The latter two were of wooden construction and subsequently demolished after a deviation was built around the Noss shipyard, completed in 1923. The line was now complete to Kingswear, and opened in August 1864, worked by the SDR. An engine shed and turntable were provided at Kingswear along with the station, all on land reclaimed from the river.

From January 1866 the Dartmouth & Torbay Railway leased itself to the South Devon Railway, and by April of that year Kingswear was ready to receive goods traffic. A further significant development during 1866 was the installation of a siding at Hollacombe (between Torquay and Paignton) for the Torquay Gas Company (see pages 42-43). This led to a steady flow of coal traffic between Kingswear and Hollacombe that continued until 1963, after which the coal came direct from the north by rail, until the gasworks closed in 1968.

In January 1872 the D&TR was fully amalgamated with the SDR, which was itself leased to the GWR from February 1876, and amalgamated with it two years later. The two-mile-long Brixham branch also started life as an independent railway, the Torbay & Brixham Railway, the personal achievement of solicitor Richard W. Wolston. Although worked by the SDR from its opening in February 1868, following a dispute with the SDR the branch company later operated its own trains until it too became part of the GWR in 1882.

Meanwhile Torquay, which already had a reputation as a health resort, had benefited greatly from the relatively early arrival of the railway in the town; the Victorian villas were spreading rapidly around the south-facing slopes of the hills, and tourist traffic was increasing. The Directors of the GWR showed an early commitment to the area by promising a prompt start on a new and much larger Torquay station, together with the doubling of the single line into Torquay. Already a separate branch track had been provided from Newton to Aller; doubling was completed to Kingskerswell during 1876 and the present Torquay station was opened in 1878, though the double track did not arrive for another four years.

The GWR also provided a Receiving Office (booking and parcels office) on the Torquay harbourside, which was as close as the railway would get to the centre of the town. Although it was in the GWR's own interest to expand its facilities to cope with the increasing traffic, another reason for this activity may have been to head off a demand for a new line to be constructed between Paignton and Totnes, so that the main line could be diverted through Torquay and so avoid the steep gradients over Dainton summit.

Further progress in doubling the line was impeded by the presence of the Livermead tunnel under Breakneck Hill near Hollacombe (see page 41), and it was to be 1910 before this had been opened out and a double track provided through to Paignton. In the meanwhile, 1892 had seen the end of the broad gauge, and with it an increase in the volume of through goods and passenger traffic from the Midlands and the North.

Beyond Hollacombe, Preston Platform opened in 1911, only to close again in 1914, but further extension of the double track was delayed until 1928, when it reached Tanners Lane, short of the then newly opened Goodrington Halt. The track through the Halt, by then renamed Goodrington Sands Halt, was doubled in 1930, but beyond this point the line has always been single, with a passing loop at Churston, although even this was removed by British Railways in 1968.

Between the wars the GWR extended the improvements it had already made to its main lines into the West Country by tackling some of the bottlenecks, such as Newton Abbot. Here a huge new station was constructed together with a new junction for the Kingswear branch at Aller, this work being completed between 1925 and 1927. Meanwhile, an extra siding had been laid on the down side of Paignton station, where additional facilities had been provided, but there was still virtually no siding capacity for terminating trains, which consequently had immediately to be worked back to Newton Abbot for servicing.

Following the completion of the new line avoiding the old wooden viaducts at Longwood and Noss, Kingswear engine shed was closed and the rolling-stock capacity of the sidings considerably increased. The timber Hoodown viaduct was also replaced, and this together with the installation of a 65-foot turntable now enabled the largest engines to come through to

Kingswear; previously the 'Torbay Express' had been booked to change engines at Torquay station in each direction. This work at the Kingswear end of the line was carried out between 1923 and 1929.

Paignton had to wait until 1930-31 for a major expansion of its capacity, when transfer of the goods traffic to a new goods shed built alongside the main road between Paignton and Goodrington enabled the platforms to be extended southwards, and for new stock sidings to be laid in the old goods yard alongside Queen's Park. This is today the site of the Paignton & Dartmouth Steam Railway station.

Further sidings were laid out alongside the new goods shed, and although this goods shed has since given way to residential flats, the sidings are still used by InterCity trains, mainly on summer Saturdays.

Construction of the magnificent new five-platform station planned for Paignton, which would have extended south well beyond Sands Road, was stopped by the war in 1939, after only preliminary works had been carried out. The Directors of the GWR were planning facilities intended to cope with the vast increase in holidaymakers to the Torbay area, which was expected to follow the advent of holidays with pay for the masses. The increased number of visitors they had envisaged certainly arrived after the war, but the staff at Paignton, from 1948 under British Railways management, had to manage as best they could without their new station.

The only part of this scheme to be resurrected after the war, and then not until 1955/56, was the elimination of the Tanners Lane level crossing at Goodrington by a road bridge, on which the present Goodrington Sands station office was built. Additional stock sidings were laid in the Clennon Valley, behind Goodrington South Sands, with locomotive turning, watering and servicing facilities, but within three years the arrival of the first main-line diesel locomotives commenced the run-down of steam working on the branch. The stock sidings still see occasional use, while the turntable was purchased by the Steam Railway and is now installed at Churston. Holiday traffic on the branch, mainly terminating at Paignton, increased steadily after the war, reaching a peak in the late 1950s, and then suffering a fairly rapid decline as the motor car and foreign holidays took their toll. Goods and parcels traffic was also in decline, but suffered a fatal blow from the Beeching Report. The 1960s consequently saw a rapid rundown in the branch infrastructure so painstakingly built up over the previous century. The Brixham branch closed in May 1963, and although the Beeching Report did not envisage the closure of the line to Kingswear, by 1968 the Paignton to Kingswear section was being proposed for closure.

Fortunately, closure did not take place before the Dart Valley Light Railway Co started negotiations for its purchase, and a shuttle service was maintained until the purchase was completed on 30 December 1972. The line had by then been reduced to a single track with only a runround loop at Kingswear.

Since then, year by year, the line has been built up again. At Paignton, Queen's Park station now stands where the Park carriage sidings were, the bay platform and sidings at Kingswear are restored, and at Churston the crossing loop, bay platform line and sidings are restored, with the addition of a turntable and, most recently, the station buildings and the new workshop on the up side.

Between Newton Abbot and Paignton the future is perhaps more in doubt, due to impending privatisation, but for the present, after the stagnation of the 1970s, the service has been improving through the 1980s, with more frequent Regional Railways local trains running through to Exeter Central and Exmouth, 'Express Sprinter' services to Cardiff and beyond, and most recently the Network SouthEast 'Sprinters' to Waterloo. InterCity presently continues to run the 'Devonian', and although the 'Torbay Express' has been relegated to a 'dated' summer service, there is still an extensive range of summer Saturday destinations. Although the density of these Saturday trains is nowhere near what it was in the peak Saturdays of the 1950s, at least their journey times and timekeeping are far better.

Lastly, I should like to thank the people who have helped me with this project, in particular Derek Frost, Alan Bennett, Bryan Gibson, Chris Mackey and the photographers who have allowed me to handle their precious material and who are each credited individually. Also the General Manager of the Paignton & Dartmouth Steam Railway, Barry Cogar, for allowing me access to the lineside in order to repeat some of the shots from the 1950s.

I hope readers will enjoy their trip down from Newton Abbot to Dartmouth, and if any of you have not already done so, that you will hasten along to make the trip yourself.

Peter W. Gray
Torquay

BIBLIOGRAPHY

Bennett, A. *GWR Holiday Lines in Devon & Somerset* (Runpast Publishing)
Cooke, R. A. *Track Layout Diagrams, Section 14: S Devon*
Hands, P. *BR Steam Shed Allocations* (Defiant Publications)
Kay, P. *Exeter-Newton Abbot - A Railway History* (Platform 5)
Langley, M. and Small, E. *Estuary & River Ferries of SW England* (Waine Research Publications)
Pike, J. R. *Iron Horse to the Sea* (Ex Libris Press)
    Torbay's Heritage - Paignton (Author & Torbay Borough Council)
Potts, C. R. *The Newton Abbot to Kingswear Railway* (The Oakwood Press)
    Scenes from the Past 19: Newton Abbot and Torbay (Foxline)
    The Brixham Branch (Oakwood Press)
Railway Correspondence & Travel Society *Locomotives of the GWR*

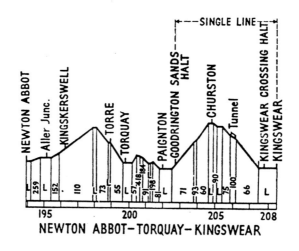

Gradient profile of the line

Newton Abbot

It is 6.27 pm on Saturday 26 July 1952 as 2-8-0 No 4708 rolls to a stand in platform Nos 1 and 2 at Newton Abbot, with the 1.25 pm from Paddington to Kingswear. This is the first part of the regular 1.30 pm from Paddington to Penzance, always known to railwaymen as 'The Dutchman', a name originating from the 'Flying Dutchman' of Broad Gauge days. But for the British Railways transfer on the tender and the red-backed numberplate, this could almost be a picture taken in Great Western days. On the side framing above the cylinder is the GWR shed code, 'OXY', indicating the engine's home depot at Oxley Sidings near Wolverhampton. The train is pure Great Western, with a Churchward 'Dreadnought' Brake 3rd leading, a typical GWR wooden post bracket signal guarding the down through line, and beyond the Loco Coal wagons contain good Welsh steam coal. *D. J. Frost*

On 13 January 1994, as 'Sprinter' unit No 150233 departs as the 15.49 to Paignton, the empty yard beyond tells its own story, the tracks have all been lifted, the sheds are deserted and nature is slowly taking over. *PWG*

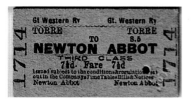

In some ways it can be shown that the railway at Newton Abbot today bears a distinct resemblance to the layout existing prior to the completion of the new station in 1927. The old station, as the first view shows (above), had only three through passenger lines and must have been very difficult to work, with all the goods traffic and the attaching and detaching of stock that was such a feature of the workings of those days. The 'Bulldog' Class 4-4-0 in the foreground appears to be backing some stock towards the station, where a 'City' Class 4-4-0 stands on the down main line. The open-cab pannier tank has a roof-boarded coach off an express train, watched by children from the railway cottages, which were subsequently destroyed in the 1940 bombing raid on the town. *PWG Collection*

In the second view (centre left), showing a busy scene on 5 July 1952, only the stone building at the rear of the Wagon Works remains from the scene of nearly 50 years earlier. 2-6-2T No 5113 is piloting 4-6-0 No 5939 *Tangley Hall* on the Plymouth portion of the 9.15 am from Liverpool, as Austerity 2-8-0 No 90176 emerges from the down through road with a load of concrete sleepers. Between the two trains can be seen a down stopper headed by a Southern Region 'West Country' Class 'Pacific', while to the right a large Prairie tank is signalled off shed. *D. J. Frost*

By 9 May 1965, the date of the third picture (opposite bottom), the DMU servicing facilities were in full use, a carriage washing plant had been installed in the old shed yard, and overhead lighting for the carriage sidings. A gantry has replaced the bracket signals controlling the down main and relief roads, though the down through line bracket signals remain. As the cross-country DMU with power car W51578 leading leaves for Penzance, the 1920s Power Station still dominates the scene, but its days are numbered too. *PWG*

The commencement of the resurgence of the West Country passenger services could be said to date from 28 January 1975, when the prototype High Speed Train set No 252001 passed through Newton Abbot to conduct trials over the South Devon banks, as seen in the fourth photograph (above). The Power Station is now partially demolished, the Wagon Works has been closed and the building taken over by publishers David & Charles, whose coaches are now on the siding alongside. The down gantry is now complete. When the resignalling of 1987 made this gantry redundant, it was lifted out and, with a few cosmetic distant arms added, now stands outside the D&C premises, just around the corner.
PWG

Finally, on 6 September 1993 (right), after the re-modelling of Newton Abbot station in 1987, we are back to three tracks through the station, though now with no shed or carriage sidings. The stone part of the old Wagon Works is now roofless, and beyond the DMU inspection sheds are disappearing into the undergrowth. The station platforms have been cut back at this end to improve the line speed for non-stop trains, and colour light signals have replaced the semaphores. In place of the relatively long stopping trains of the 1950s, we now have the more frequent two-car 'Sprinter' sets, such as this unit No 150233 on the 14.45 Exmouth to Paignton service. *PWG*

This pair of pictures says it all for Newton Abbot. On 5 November 1960 passengers aboard the up 'Cornish Riviera Express' are taking their lunch in the elegant splendour of ex-GWR restaurant car No W9623W, which is paired with No W9617W. One of the signalmen in West box looks out to see that all is well, as the 'Limited' accelerates up through the station behind a 'Warship' Class diesel-hydraulic locomotive, after dropping the steam pilot engine, which is now sitting in platform No 8. In the background, the DMU inspection sheds have already been erected, while the coal stage attached to the steam shed has been demolished to make room for the new diesel maintenance shed. The steam engines are now being coaled by two grab cranes.

Today provision for the motor car has taken over the old up through and main lines, as Class '47' No 47844, bearing the rather unwieldy name *Derby & Derbyshire Chamber of Commerce & Industry*, leaves for Paignton on 4 September 1993 with the 10.05 from York. The forest developing in the old shed yard is beginning to envelop the shell of the old engine shed and Locomotive Factory, where all is dereliction and decay. This site once gave employment to over 1,000 men and a few women; now only a handful are needed to run the remaining services at Newton Abbot. *Both PWG*

On principal Express trains of British Railways
there are

RESTAURANT CARS

OR BUFFET CARS

in which meals or snacks can be enjoyed
en route at popular prices.

From the BR Holiday Guide, 1951.

Aller Junction

From Newton Abbot out to Aller, the Kingswear branch tracks run alongside those of the main line, which then turn away to the west. There have been four tracks on this section since 1877, but there was no physical junction between them at Aller until 1925, when the track layout was altered in connection with the rebuilding of Newton Abbot station. Reading from the left, the tracks then became Up Main, Up Relief, Down Main and Down Relief, on which '5101' Class 2-6-2T No 4178 is hauling the through Cardiff to Paignton coaches off the 11.10 am Swansea to Penzance train on 20 September 1959. *PWG*

In the early 1960s the old GWR wooden post bracket signals were replaced by a metal gantry carrying the same six semaphore indications, controlling movements over the crossovers between the down lines, and also access to the down goods loop added at the foot of Dainton bank in 1941. On 25 September 1971, the date of the second view (above right), with Class '47' No 1656 passing with the 12.30 from Paddington to Penzance, a number of other alterations have taken place. The telegraph poles on the up side and their associated wires have all been put into ground-level troughing. The up line semaphore signals have been converted to colour lights, and the ramps for the GWR Automatic Train Control apparatus resited to a position almost opposite the gantry. The down main line and the main Torquay road alongside have both acquired 40 mph restriction signs. *D. H. Mitchell*

Following the elimination of Aller Junction in 1987, the tracks have now reverted to their pre-1925 sequence of up and down main line and up and down branch line, with the junctions now on the section between the far end of this straight and the cutting leading into Newton Abbot station. The branch colour light signal is almost back in the position of the GWR wooden post as 'Express Sprinter' No 158820 approaches with today's equivalent of the 1959 train, the 13.00 from Cardiff to Paignton on 13 January 1994 (right). Noticeable in the 1994 view is the untidy effect created by the mixture of dark and light coloured ballast stone, and the loss of the neat edge to the ballast shoulder with present-day mechanical maintenance. Note also the increase in road traffic, which is often nose-to-tail for long periods on this section. *PWG*

Looking in the other direction from the same bridge, we see Aller Junction itself, with the 46-lever signal box of 1925 hiding behind the first telegraph pole (above left). On the far right can be seen the Dainton banker, a '5101' Class 2-6-2T, sitting in the banker spur, beneath the water tank. The train is the 6.10 pm from Goodrington Sands Halt to Plymouth, a 'dated' service making its last run for 1960 on 26 August. The locomotive is something of a rarity for Devon, 4-6-0 No 7819 *Hinton Manor* from Oswestry (89A), possibly returning from Paignton after working a Friday relief train down from Shrewsbury. She will be replaced at Newton Abbot by 4-6-0 No 6988 *Swithland Hall*, joining the other end of the train for the non-stop run down to Plymouth. *PWG*

By 4 June 1983 (left) we have a better view of the signal box, as Class '33s' Nos 33106 and 33027 *Earl Mountbatten of Burma* return through Aller Junction with an Ian Allan special train, the 'Torbay Express' from Waterloo to Kingswear. The signalman now has a car parked outside the box, and the railway allotments on the left, so industriously tended in 1960, are now partially abandoned. *R. W. Penny*

The Aller junctions were lifted in 1987, and the box was closed and demolished. In 1993 (above) a 13-coach up train from Paignton is passing the junction site, clear of the Plymouth lines. This was a returning charter special, the 17.46 from Paignton to Cambridge, on 21 August, travelling behind green-liveried Class '47' No D1962 (47833) *Captain Peter Manisty RN*. The allotments are now a jungle, over which even the Torquay Road lighting columns can only just peer - all to be swept away when work starts on the Kingskerswell bypass in the not too distant future. *PWG*

1932 excursion leaflet

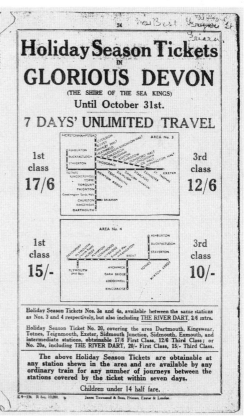

19

The first overbridge on the branch proper crosses the line less than half a mile beyond Aller, and the row of houses adjacent to the junction can be seen behind the telegraph poles on the left as 4-6-0 No 5038 *Morlais Castle*, which has worked the 10.45 am Manchester to Plymouth train between Shrewsbury and Newton Abbot, now takes the branch portion on to Kingswear. The tree-lined slopes in the background conceal a huge sand quarry, for which a siding was laid on the down side at Aller in 1866. It was removed 100 years later, though in latter years it had been mainly used for storing 'cripple' stock awaiting attention in the Wagon Works. *PWG*

When *Morlais Castle* passed on its way to Kingswear, the overbridge had carried a quiet country lane, but by 1984 the railway connection to Stoneycombe quarry had been removed and this lane then became the main access route to the quarry; the 'improved' junction with the main road can be seen in the background. Meanwhile, the 'Torbay Express' name had been re-introduced in 1983 for the 09.20 Paddington to Paignton HST service, but in 1984 this reverted to a locomotive and stock working. For the inaugural service on 14 May 1984 an immaculate Class '50', No 50003 *Temeraire*, was provided, carrying a 'Torbay Express' headboard on the 10.35 Paddington to Paignton service. The headboard survived only for the first two months, even then being carried only intermittently. *R. W. Penny*

Today one almost takes one's life in one's hand to photograph a train here, as lorry after lorry cross the bridge, often queuing to let each other pass. There is no longer the same problem with the trains, as they trundle at a sedate 40 mph towards Kingskerswell. This is the 13.00 from Cardiff to Paignton again, reduced to a 'Sprinter', No 150261, on 17 January 1994. *PWG*

A very noticeable feature of the pictures taken recently along the BR section of the branch is the vast increase in the amount of vegetation, not just on the lineside banks but everywhere, when compared with 30 years ago. Possibly the run of very mild winters recently has had this effect. Granted the first picture of this pair was taken in the winter, as B-B 'Warship' Class diesel-hydraulic No D823 *Hermes* takes the down 'Torbay Express' along the valley towards Kingskerswell, but the contrast with this summer's picture is striking. *D. J. Frost*

On 19 August 1993 'Sprinter' No 150230 is operating one of the very useful through services from Exmouth to Paignton, via the centre of Exeter, this one departing Exmouth at 14.45. *PWG*

Kingskerswell

Looking towards Kingskerswell station (above), which can be seen through the arch of the road bridge spanning the valley, 'Castle' Class 4-6-0 No 5074 *Hampden* is bringing the evening goods up from Goodrington to Newton Abbot on 4 July 1958. This was a regular duty for the engine off the down 'Torbay Express', and the headboard is stowed on the spare lamp bracket. In the foreground is the fogman's hut with brazier standing alongside the Kingskerswell starting signal, just out of the picture, which also carried the Aller distant signal.

Although the vegetation seems not to have increased very much between 1958 and 1970, the date of the second view (above right), there has been some development of the foreground 'business', and a colour light signal has replaced the semaphore Aller distant, Kingskerswell box being now closed and demolished as C-C 'Western' Class diesel-hydraulic No 1005 *Western Venturer* sweeps around the curve with the summer Saturday 15.40 Paignton to Sheffield.

There does, however, seem to have been a major increase in the level of growth during the last 20 years, as can be seen in the third photograph (right) taken on 19 August 1993. The 'business' having developed still further is now ringed with trees, making the previous viewpoint unavailable, as 'Sprinter Express' No 158829 makes the outward run of a short working, the 16.00 from Paignton to Newton Abbot. *All PWG*

Kingskerswell station when it opened in 1853 consisted only of a very short wooden platform on this (up) side of the single broad gauge line. A down platform was provided when the line was doubled in 1876, access being obtained by knocking down part of the bridge parapet, below which the fine wooden steps took the passenger down to platform level. In this picture we are looking towards Newton Abbot as the 9.05 am Swansea to Kingswear drifts into the station at 3.31 pm on Saturday 5 August 1961. On summer Saturdays in post-war steam days, all local trains were suspended from around 10.30 am until the evening, in order to keep the line clear for the holiday trains. Consequently local passengers had a very meagre service from Kingskerswell in 1961, with only this train and another an hour later booked to stop. The steps to reach the up platform were contained within the station building which can just be seen on the left, tucked into the corner of the bridge.

Kingskerswell station and its signal box both closed in 1964, but the platforms are still in place, and there is talk of re-opening it. Meanwhile, the bridge has almost been restored to its pre-1876 condition as the latest in BR air-conditioned stock rolls under and climbs towards Torquay, No 158829 forming the 13.00 Cardiff to Paignton service on 19 August 1993. *Both PWG*

Trips on the river Dart have been popular ever since the railway opened, and whole excursion trains were often devoted to this service. This one originated from Torrington in North Devon, and after dropping its passengers at Totnes in the morning has subsequently run as empty stock back to Newton Abbot and then down to Kingswear, where the return journey commenced. These and other excursions were normally the only trains that brought Southern Region engines on to the Kingswear branch and this one, returning through Kingskerswell station on 26 June 1959, viewed from the top of the wooden steps, is hauled by 2-6-2T No 5178 and 'West Country' 'Pacific' No 34033 *Chard*.

Today's equivalent must be the Network SouthEast Class '159' three-car sets that commenced regular services to Paignton in July 1993. The Kingskerswell station site looks rather forlorn as No 159006 runs through on its way to Southampton with the 15.46 service from Paignton on 31 July 1993. *PWG*

From Kingskerswell it is a steady climb at 1 in 110 to the summit near Lawes Bridge on the outskirts of Torquay. BR Standard '7MT' 4-6-2 No 70018 *Flying Dutchman* is approaching Toby Cottage (since demolished), by the bridle path to Edginswell, with the 10.40 am Paddington to Paignton on 19 July 1952. *D. J. Frost*

The only problem this climb presents to the HST sets is that of keeping their speed down to the 40 mph line speed limit, caused by cash-limited maintenance to rather elderly chaired track. It is noticeable that the 1952 fencing has now been swallowed up by the undergrowth, as Power Car No 43082 leads the 08.05 service from Newcastle to Paignton on 31 July 1993. The footbridge from which this picture was taken is part of a longer footbridge that once spanned the tracks at Dawlish Warren. *PWG*

Almost exactly 40 years separate these two views of trains breasting the summit between Kingskerswell and Torre. This is where Brunel placed the Pumping House for the planned Atmospheric System of train working. However, although the building was completed, the engines that had been ordered from Boulton & Watt were never installed, as three months prior to opening the South Devon Railway decided to abandon the Atmospheric System in favour of locomotive haulage. It is nevertheless still the most complete of the three remaining Pumping Houses and the only one to retain its Italianate chimney. On Sunday 16 August 1953 the area is still almost virgin country-side as 2-6-2T No 5551 hurries the 9.30 am from Moretonhampstead to Goodrington Sands Halt south to the seaside.

However, 40 years later on Saturday 21 August 1993 the scene has changed somewhat as Power Car No 43048 leads the 06.13 from Derby down to Paignton. Only in the last two years has development commenced to the north (right in this picture) of the railway, already including a dual-carriageway road, superstores and housing that will soon cover the background hills.
Both PWG

Trains leaving Torquay in the up direction face a steady climb all the way to Lawes Bridge - about 1½ miles at 1 in 55 and 1 in 73. Consequently in steam days their speed at the summit was often quite low, even if they had taken banking assistance from Torquay up to Torre. On Saturday 22 August 1953 4-6-0 No 4079 *Pendennis Castle* lifts the 10.20 am from Kingswear to Manchester (and Liverpool) up to the summit at a steady pace, though not with the consummate ease displayed by the Class '47' on the same train 40 years later, the 09.55 Paignton to Manchester on 28 August 1993. *Both PWG*

For a period during the mid-1950s it was normal practice for a pair of tank engines to work the 'Devonian' express, the 9.15 am from Paignton to Bradford (Forster Square), over the first section of its journey as far as Newton Abbot. With the full 12-coach load, the 'Castle' Class 4-6-0 that normally took the train on to Bristol would certainly have required assistance on the climb out of Torquay, which this pair of BR Standard Class '3MT' 2-6-2Ts, Nos 82005 and 82009, are taking in their stride in the early summer of 1956. *B. B. Williams*

Also climbing effortlessly past the site of the old Devon General bus garage is Class '47' No 47816 on the 08.39 Paignton to Glasgow service on 4 September 1993. Two months later it might be a different story as the lineside forest deposits its leaves on the line. Regional Railways had no money for any cutting back during the summer of 1993, and it shows. *PWG*

Torre

It being a dull and drizzly day on Saturday 26 April 1958, I walked down to Torre station intending to catch a train to Exeter, only to discover that there had been an accident there that morning. The locomotive on the 8.55 am Newton Abbot to Kingswear train, 4-6-0 No 7004 *Eastnor Castle*, had run through adverse signals approaching Torre and collided with the rear of a two-wagon goods train hauled by 0-6-0T No 9668, which was standing on the down line. Fortunately, the wooden wagon next to the brake van took much of the force of the collision and no one was hurt, although *Eastnor Castle* suffered a badly bent front end. By the time this picture was taken, the 'Castle' had been removed to the coal yard, mostly empty of wagons on a Saturday, and the Newton Abbot breakdown crane was lifting the badly damaged brake van clear of the running line.

Today's picture, taken on 16 January 1994, shows the running lines still in place, but little else. The tracks into the goods shed (foreground roof) and into the coal yard were all lifted during the period 1967-69, and only one building remains from the four coal merchants trading there in 1958. *Both PWG*

As many readers will remember, the winter of 1962-3 was a particularly hard one, and snow is falling on Torre station as a B-B diesel-hydraulic 'D63XX' locomotive prepares to depart for Goodrington after leaving Torre traffic from the 8.15 am ex-Hackney Yard, Newton Abbot, on 11 February 1963. There is still plenty of goods traffic in the yard, and on the up platform one of the staff waits for the 9.25 am from Paignton to Bradford, the 'Devonian', which is due in two minutes' time. The passengers are probably huddling in the shelter of the roofed footbridge, because the up-side buildings had recently been demolished and work on the replacement shelter had been suspended because of the freezing weather.

At first glance Torre may not look much changed today, but it is now an unstaffed halt, and the down-side buildings, extended across the platform, are now an antiques emporium. The signal box remains, in a preserved condition but disconnected from the real railway. The goods shed on the down side closed in 1965, and the remainder of the coal traffic was terminated in 1967. However, there has been a welcome increase in passenger traffic, in part due to the improved service, which has increased from 14 down trains in 1983 to 20 in the 1993-4 winter timetable, Mondays to Fridays. This includes some longer-distance 'Sprinter' services such as the 09.30 from Bristol via Exeter Central, seen arriving on 10 November 1993. *Both PWG*

The largest crane at Torre, a hand-operated 10-ton machine, was located in the small yard at the Torquay end, adjacent to the main road. In 1907, using this crane, the cars for the Torquay Electric Tramways were unloaded from the flat trucks on which they arrived, on to horse-drawn drays for transport across town to the depot at Plainmoor. They were built by Brush of Loughborough, and Car No 7 has just been lifted from the flat truck in the background, which stands in front of the awning seen on the right of the picture on the previous page. *PWG Collection*

An industrial building and car sales occupy the same area today, and the station footbridge can be seen in the background of this view taken on 16 January 1994. Two of the town's three initial tram routes started from outside Torre station, and although abandoned in 1934, a short length of track still lies in the road outside the station, though now buried several inches below the tarmac surface. *PWG*

Below right is an advert from a 1922 guide to Paignton.

Torquay Tramways Co., Ltd.

CIRCULAR TOUR

From Paignton through Torquay & Babbacombe   Fare **9d.**

Cars at intervals as advertised in the Company's Official Time Tables, price ½d. from any Conductor.

CARS

at Frequent Intervals from Paignton

(CHANGE AT TORQUAY)

to the following Places of Interest :

CHAPEL HILL (Pine Wood and Ancient Chapel).
ANSTEY'S COVE (Tea, Boating, Fishing, Bathing).
KENT'S CAVERN (Prehistoric Dwelling Place).
BABBACOMBE DOWNS (Magnificent Scenery).
PETITTOR (18-hole Golf Course).
TORRE STATION (for Chapel Hill).
ST. MARY CHURCH for WATCOMBE.
WELLSWOOD (for Kent's Cavern).
COCKINGTON (Famous Forge and Village).

2

On a rather dull day, the driver of 4-6-0 No 7029 *Clun Castle*, although nearly halfway along the short platform, has only just closed the regulator, allowing the first seven coaches of the 'Devonian' to come to rest at Torre on 25 November 1961. On the right the station nameboard is missing, possibly while the lettering was being altered from 'Torre for St Marychurch and Babbacombe', a reference to one of the tram routes, to plain 'Torre'. On the down platform a large number of station barrows are awaiting disposal; many once used for the milk churn traffic had been kept for the use of the newspaper wholesaler, who had them to divide up his stock as it came off the early morning newspaper train.

In the second view Class '47' No 47853 powers through Torre with the non-stop 09.55 Paignton to Manchester on 4 September 1993. The nameboard is back, but the wagons in the coal yard have gone, as has the siding into the goods yard where the trams were unloaded. *Both PWG*

A signal event in 1957 was the appearance on the branch of the celebrated GWR 4-4-0 No 3440 *City of Truro*, making her first long-distance excursion since being put back into running order at Swindon, after many years in the old railway museum at York. The excursion ran from Swindon to Kingswear and is here seen climbing the 1 in 55 bank from Torquay to Torre on the return journey, assisted by 2-6-2T No 4179 on Sunday 19 May 1957. *B. B. Williams*

The afternoon of 18 September 1993 saw the relatively unusual sight of the 16.11 from Paignton to Liverpool being hauled out of Torquay by Class '37' No 37263 in the Civil Engineer's livery. The Class '47' that had brought the train down had failed in Goodrington yard, and No 37263, the Newton Abbot stand-by locomotive that day, had been summoned to bring the train back. *PWG*

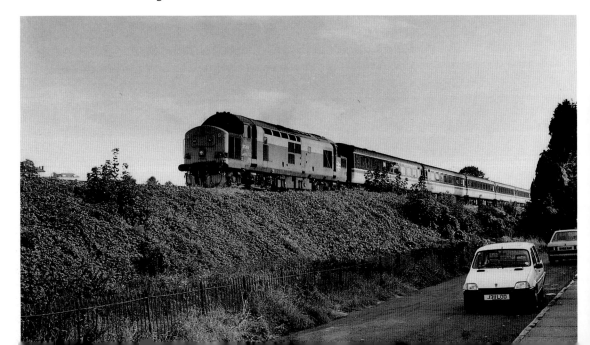

Torquay

In steam days the 1 in 55 gradient from the end of Torquay platform up to Torre, and the 1 in 73 beyond, meant that the use of a banking engine was essential for trains over ten coaches in length, and sometimes for lesser loads according to the power provided at the front end. On 28 June 1952 Newton Abbot's 2-6-2T No 4547, still in green with 'GWR' on her tanksides, is running bunker-first banking 4-6-0 No 5992 *Horton Hall* with 12 coaches bound for Bradford.

Extracts from the February 1947 GWR Exeter Division Appendix regarding the incline between Torquay and Torre.

SECTIONS OF LINE OVER WHICH PASSENGER, COACHING STOCK, PERISHABLE, AND PARCELS TRAINS MAY BE ASSISTED IN THE REAR IN CLEAR WEATHER.

Section.	Distance.	Gradient.	Whether Assistant Engine to run in rear coupled or uncoupled.
	M. C.		
Torquay to Torre ..	1 20	Rising all the way, Ruling gradient 1 in 55.	To run uncoupled, unless Train is booked to call at Torre, in which case Engine to run coupled as far as Torre Station and be uncoupled there. The Assistant Engine to come to the rear of the Train whilst it is standing at Torquay Up Platform. The Assistant Engine must not proceed beyond the Torre Up Outer Advanced Starting Signal, but must wait there until verbally instructed to return to Torre Station, or until the Train has cleared the Signal Box in advance and the Outer Advanced Starting Signal has again been lowered for the Engine to proceed. During fog or falling snow, the Assistant Engine must not run in the rear of a Train, but must be coupled in front, in which case it must proceed through to Newton Abbot and the Train (if not booked to call at that Station) must be brought to a stand at Newton Abbot West Box Up Home Signal for the Assistant Engine to be detached.

Working of Freight Trains down Inclines between Torre and Torquay.

Down Freight Trains not stopping at Torre may proceed direct to Torquay after putting down brakes at the stop board situated at 218m. 26ch. without stopping to pick up and set down brakes at the intermediate stop board near the water column at Torre.

Drivers must satisfy themselves before proceeding that sufficient brakes have been applied to control the train on the gradient between Torre and Torquay.

Most of the more recent Saturday long-distance trains have arrived with their own built-in bankers, and here, also by the Walnut Road overbridge, Power Car No 43051 *The Duke and Duchess of York* is assisting No 43085 *City of Bradford* with the 06.13 from Derby to Penzance, which included a trip down to Paignton and back in its itinerary on 4 September 1993. *Both PWG*

Above On summer Saturdays Torquay North signal box, on the other side of the Walnut Road overbridge from the photographs on the previous page and in reality a ground frame released by the main signal box at the south end of the station, sprung to life to operate the facing crossover under the bridge, used by the two London-bound trains that started from Torquay. Unless it had a very short train, 2-6-0 No 9306 on the 10.55 am Paignton to Nottingham is probably being banked up to Torre on 5 September 1953. *D. J. Frost*

Below Today the vegetation has taken over completely, as an HST set runs empty down into Torquay bound for a return working from Paignton later on 4 September 1993. *PWG*

Below right Tempting holidaymakers to Torquay - from *Shire of the Sea Kings*, 1912 edition, *Holidays by LMS* in the 1920s, the BR *Holiday Guide* of 1951, and *Holiday Haunts* of 1959.

Ideal Resort FOR HEALTH AND PLEASURE.
MAGNIFICENT SCENERY.
SAFE BATHING.
Within easy distance of the Wilds of Dartmoor.

Owing to . . . . .
Unique Position . .
Summer . . .
Temperature
Cool. .

TORQUAY

. . HIGHEST

. . . WINTER SUNSHINE

Marine and Moorland Excursions. Golf and Bowling. Theatre, Bands, Concerts, Promenade Piers. Splendid Train Service. Good Hotels, Boarding Houses and Apartments.
ILLUSTRATED DESCRIPTIVE BOOK FREE ON APPLICATION TO
FREDK. S. HEX, *Town Clerk*.

Above The scene again in 1972, with only the foundations of the signal box remaining, as a 'Western' Class diesel-hydraulic hauls 2-6-2T No 4555 and the Dart Valley Railway train back to Totnes, after their day of trial running between Paignton and Kingswear on 30 July. *PWG*

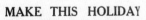

Torquay station displays the wide clearance between its three tracks that denote a station opened in broad gauge days, in 1878, although the extended platforms and bays at this northern end of the site did not appear until the late 1920s. The bay platforms had been used before the war for attaching extra coaches to the front of the 'Torbay Express', and latterly for theatrical traffic and the triennial visit by the Bertram Mills Circus trains, but it was most unusual to find a locomotive there. This was Tuesday 28 July 1959, the second day of official 'dieselisation' of the 'Torbay Express', and the diesel booked for this working had been used by Newton Abbot to replace failed North British engine No D603 *Conquest* on an early Plymouth to London train. 4-6-0 No 5032 *Usk Castle* was sent down to Kingswear with headboard ready to work the 'Torbay Express' to London, but 'Warship' Class D805 *Benbow* became available at the last moment and took over from *Usk Castle* at Torquay. The 'Castle' then followed 'light engine' back to Newton Abbot. *B. B. Williams*

A block of flats now occupies the site of the bay platforms, and although the station buildings are not altered externally, the up-side buildings are now no longer used by the railway. Power Cars Nos 43087 and 43198 idle while passenger board the 09.15 Paignton to Newcastle on 4 September 1993. *PWG*

Sketch map of Torquay station in the early 1960s.

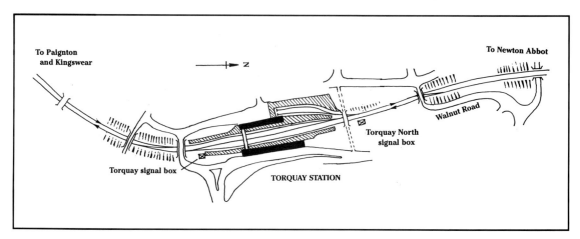

To Paignton and Kingswear

N

To Newton Abbot

Walnut Road

Torquay North signal box

Torquay signal box

TORQUAY STATION

The '45XX' Class 2-6-2Ts were strong little engines, as No 4566 is about to demonstrate, leaving the south end of Torquay station for Paignton with the eight-coach 8.10 pm from Newton Abbot on 20 July 1960. A few days earlier No 4566 had been the official last steam engine to be repaired at the Newton Abbot Locomotive Factory, and is 'running in' prior to returning to her home depot at Penzance. Before the platforms were lengthened in the late 1920s, there had been sidings off a wagon turntable between the station and the signal box.

Apart from the closure of the signal box, removal of the middle road and the awning extension on the down side, not too much has changed in 1993 as Power Car No 43102 prepares to head the 08.05 from Newcastle on the final stage of its journey to Paignton on 4 September. Certainly the latest style of lighting column is a considerable improvement on the concrete ones erected as part of the 1955 Modernisation Plan. *Both PWG*

The down 'Torbay Express' leaves Torquay, with the leading coaches crossing the Cockington Lane bridge, hauled by 'Warship' Class D808 *Centaur*, probably on 27 July 1959, the first official day for diesel-hydraulic haulage (above). The signals, which are, in the distance, the Torquay advanced starter and, on the left, the Torquay Gas Works signal box down distant, were to be vital witnesses to an accident that occurred here three years later. *B. B. Williams*

On 25 August 1962 D833 *Panther*, hauling the 10.15 am Paddington to Kingswear, managed to get only a little further than D808 above, when it failed, with its last coach on the Cockington Lane bridge. The driver of the following train, the 7.45 am Paddington to Paignton (via Bristol), hauled by 4-6-0 No 4932 *Hatherton Hall*, failed to observe the advanced starter at danger and almost immediately ran into the back of the first train. The Gas Works distant was, of course, still 'off' for the first train. The second view (centre) shows the scene after the undamaged coaches from the first train had been removed to Paignton. *L. F. Folkard*

A scene not greatly changed today (left), as Class '47' No 47810 advances rapidly across the Cockington Lane bridge with the 09.18 Manchester to Paignton on 2 October 1993. *PWG*

It was this single line tunnel under Breakneck Hill between Livermead and Hollacombe that prevented the doubling of the line through to Paignton before 1910. Bursting out of it, on a train bound for Kingswear, is one of the then almost new '45XX' Class 2-6-2Ts, then numbered from 2161 upwards. *PWG Collection*

In this identical 1993 view, the last vestige of the tunnel mouth can still be seen, just ahead of Power Car No 43056 *University of Bradford*, heading the 11.45 Paddington to Paignton, with No 43044 *Borough of Kettering* bringing up the rear on 2 October 1993. *PWG*

Paignton

Before the arrival of North Sea Gas, a familiar, if unwelcome, sight, was the Torquay & Paignton Gas Works, situated above Hollacombe beach on the border between the two towns. Repainted Collett 0-6-0 No 2275 from Taunton, probably on a 'running in' turn after a spell in the Newton Abbot Locomotive Factory, shunts the loaded wagons alongside the retort house, still covered in wartime camouflage paint (above left). *D. J. Frost*

In the second view (below left), taken some years later, a lone blue Class '47' makes it way down to Paignton. The signal box and gasworks have gone, but the sidings and gasholders remain. *A. Hill*

On 28 August 1993 (above) Power Cars Nos 43074 and 43059 are returning the 06.13 from Derby to Newton Abbot, so that after visiting Paignton it can resume its journey to Penzance. Some rather unkempt greenery covers the railway side of the site, but beyond this the Borough of Torbay has created a beautiful park, with circular ponds where the gasholders once stood. *PWG*

Below is an extract from the 1947 GWR Exeter Division Appendix regarding shunting the gasworks siding and using the wagon tippler.

GAS HOUSE SIDING.
Shunting.

Whenever a Freight train worked by one Guard has to perform work at this Siding, a Porter must be sent from Torquay to assist.

Wagon Tippler.

The following restrictions must be observed in connection with the wagon tippler in use at this Siding, and coal traffic to the Siding must only be loaded in wagons that can be tipped:

No wagon with a greater length of body than 18 feet 6 inches and a depth exceeding 6 feet and less than 3 feet can be tipped.

The maximum lifting capacity is a loaded 12-ton coal wagon.

To avoid loss of oil, grease box wagons should as far as possible be loaded to the Siding, but if any wagons fitted with oil axle boxes (other than the standard 12-ton boxes) are used, they must, after tipping, be specially labelled for the axle boxes to be replenished with oil.

On 4 September 1954 4-6-0 No 5949 *Trematon Hall* runs into Paignton station across the level crossing with the 6.40 am from Leicester to Paignton (top), while 4-6-0 No 6821 *Leaton Grange* waits to leave with train number 545, the 2.45 pm from Paignton to Paddington (a list of the Up Train Reporting Numbers for 1954 is given opposite and overleaf). The bell mounted on the signal post on the right gave warning when the gates were about to move. The station nameboard is the original GWR version, still backed by enamel advertising signs attached to the fencing. *PWG*

In the late 1960s (above) the 'Picture House' has become a 'Cinema', the nameboard has acquired BR-style lettering and the enamel signs have gone. The motive power has also changed, as 'Warship' Class diesel-hydraulic No 855 *Triumph* passes 'Peak' Class diesel-electric No 182 waiting at the platform. *A. Hill*

The advertisement is from *Holiday Haunts*, 1959.

By 1993 shorter trains have enabled the starting signal to be placed further from the crossing, which is now a lifting barrier, and the timber rear wall below the platform awning has been replaced with a white paling fence. Through this can be seen the Paignton & Dartmouth Steam Railway station and some of their stock, including just the top of 4-6-0 No 4920 *Dumbleton Hall*, standing outside the 'Picture House' which is also now owned by the Steam Railway. Incidentally, this lays claim to being the oldest purpose-built working picture theatre in Western Europe. Leading the 10.45 from Paddington into Paignton is Power Car No 43179 *Pride of Laira*, while the outgoing train is the 14.05 to Paddington led by Power Car No 43029. *PWG*

Below and overleaf Train Reporting Numbers for up trains from the Exeter Division, Summer 1954.

SECTION—WEST OF ENGLAND TO PADDINGTON.
(TRAINS STARTING FROM EXETER DISTRICT.)

500	7. 0 a.m.	Kingswear **R K**	Paddington	..	Saturdays	Kingswear	..	Newton Abbot.
505	8. 0 a.m.	,, **R**	,,		,,			
508	9. 5 a.m.	Minehead ..	,,	..	Saturdays, 3rd July– 11th September.	Taunton	..	Paddington.
510	9.45 a.m.	Churston R ..	,,	..	Saturdays.			
513	10.40 a.m.	Minehead ..	,,	..	,,	,,	..	,,
515	10.35 a.m.	Torquay R ..	,,	..	,,			
520	11.20 a.m.	Kingswear R ..	,,	..	,,			
520	11.25 a.m.	,,	,,	..	**Mondays to Fridays**			
522	11.50 a.m.	Minehead ..	,,	..	Saturdays.	,,	..	,,
525	11.30 a.m.	Torquay R ..	,,	..	,, .			
528	12.18 p.m.	Newton Abbot	,,	..	,,			
530	1.30 p.m.	Paignton R ..	,,	..	Saturdays, 10th July– 28th August.			
535	1.40 p.m.	Kingswear R ..	,,	..	Saturdays.			
540	1.45 p.m.	Paignton R ..	,,	..	Saturdays, 26th June –3rd July and 4th to 18th Sept.			
540	1.55 p.m.	Torquay R ..	,,	..	Saturdays, 10th July– 28th August.			
542	2.15 p.m.	Minehead ..	,,	..	Saturdays to 11th September.	,,	..	,,
545	2.45 p.m.	Paignton R ..	,,	..	Saturdays to 4th September.			
550	4.15 p.m.	Paignton R ..	,,	..	Saturdays.			
555	4.35 p.m.	Kingswear R ..	,,	..	,,			

K—Kingswear–Paddington portion connecting with the 7.0 a.m. Plymouth (North Road) at Newton Abbot.
R—Block Reservation Train.

Train No.	Time.	Train. From	Train. To	Days Number to be carried.	No. carried throughout Journey (except where otherwise shewn). From	No. carried throughout Journey (except where otherwise shewn). To

SECTION—WEST OF ENGLAND TO BRISTOL AND TO L.M.R. (MIDLAND SECTION).
(TRAINS STARTING FROM EXETER DISTRICT.)

Train No.	Time.	From	To	Days Number to be carried.	From	To
523	6.55 a.m.	Paignton R ..	Sheffield ..	Saturdays	Paignton ..	Bristol (T.M.).
533	7.45 a.m.	,, R ..	Newcastle ..	Saturdays, 3rd July–18th September.	,, ..	St. Philip's Marsh.
543	8.40 a.m.	,, R ..	Nottingham ..	Saturdays to 11th September.	,, ..	,, ,,
547	12. 5 p.m.	,,	Bristol (T.M.)	Saturdays, 3rd July–24th July and 4th September.		
553	8.52 a.m.	,, R ..	Sheffield N ..	Saturdays to 11th September.	,, ..	Bristol (T.M.).
563	8.45 a.m.	Kingswear R ..	Bradford ..	Saturdays	Kingswear ..	St. Philip's Marsh.
552	10.15 a.m.	Teignmouth ..	,, ..	,, ...	Teignmouth ..	,, ,,
573	10.58 a.m.	Paignton R ..	Nottingham ..	,, ...	Paignton ..	,, ,,
583	2.25 p.m.	,, R ..	Derby ..	Saturdays, 3rd July–14th August.	,, ..	,, ,,
593	5.15 p.m.	,, R ..	Nottingham ..	Saturdays, 19th June–4th September.	,, ..	Bristol (T.M.).

SECTION—WEST OF ENGLAND TO BIRMINGHAM AND WOLVERHAMPTON.
VIA STRATFORD-UPON-AVON.
(TRAINS STARTING FROM EXETER DISTRICT.)

Train No.	Time.	From	To	Days Number to be carried.	From	To
527	10. 0 a.m.	Torquay R ..	Wolverhampton (via Oxford)	Saturdays, 10th July–4th September.		
537	10.35 a.m.	Paignton R ..	Wolverhampton	Saturdays.		
547	12. 5 p.m.	,, R ..	Birmingham (Moor St.)	Saturdays, 31st July 28th Aug.		
557	12.15 p.m.	Kingswear R ..	,, ,,	Saturdays.		
560	10.55 a.m.	Ilfracombe ..	Birmingham (S.H.)	,,	Taunton ..	Birmingham (S.H.).
567	1.55 p.m.	Paignton R ..	Wolverhampton	Saturdays, 24th July–7th August.		
577	2.55 p.m.	,, R ..	Wolverhampton	Saturdays, 26th June–4th September.		
587	3. 5 p.m.	,, R ..	,,	Saturdays, 19th June and 11th and 18th September.		
587	3.10 p.m.	,, R ..	,,	Saturdays, 26th June–4th September.		

SECTION—WEST OF ENGLAND TO NORTH VIA SEVERN TUNNEL AND TO SOUTH WALES.
(TRAINS STARTING FROM EXETER DISTRICT.)

Train No.	Time.	From	To	Days Number to be carried.	From	To
570	7.45 a.m.	Newton Abbot ..	Swansea (H.S.)	Saturdays ..	Newton Abbot ..	Cardiff (Gen.).
574	8.25 a.m.	Ilfracombe ..	Manchester (Exchange)K	, ...	Taunton ..	Shrewsbury.
575	10. 4 a.m.	Exeter (St. D.)	Manchester (London Rd.)	,, ...	Exeter (St. D.)	,,
578	8. 5 a.m.	Paignton ..	Manchester (Victoria)	Saturdays, 26th June–28th August.	Paignton ..	,,
579	9. 5 a.m.	,,	Manchester (London Rd.)	Saturdays	,, ..	,,
580	9. 5 a.m.	Kingswear ..	Swansea (High Street)	Saturdays, 3rd July–11th September.		
585	10.10 a.m.	Paignton ..	Cardiff (Gen.)	Saturdays.		
588	9.25 a.m.	Ilfracombe ..	,, ,,	,, ...	Taunton ..	Cardiff (Gen.).
590	10.20 a.m.	Kingswear ..	Crewe ..	,, ...	Kingswear ..	Pontypool Road.
594	12.30 p.m.	Paignton ..	Manchester (London Rd.)	,, ...	Paignton ..	Shrewsbury.
595	3.20 p.m.	Kingswear ..	Cardiff (Gen.)	,,		

K—Terminates at Bristol (T.M.) Saturdays, 19th and 26th June, inclusive.
N—To Leeds, Saturdays, 10th July to 28th August, inclusive.
R—Block Reservation Train.

The old footbridge across the railway at Paignton, adjacent to Paignton North Box, formed a suitable triumphal arch for trains entering the station over the busy Torbay Road level crossing. From it there was a fine view of the station, and of trains approaching from Kingswear, which did not stop until their buffers were very close to the gates. Indeed, it was normal practice to open the gates even though the signal was at danger, in case one overran ever so slightly. *R. W. Penny*

The footbridge seen from the station platform. The original Woolworths building, barely visible behind 4-6-0 No 4967 *Shirenewton Hall*, was more in scale with the other main street buildings than the one that replaced it. However, there were operating problems on 5 August 1961, and most trains were running late; *Shirenewton Hall*'s train, the 10.20 am from Kingswear to Manchester, had been held out at Goodrington and did not arrive at Paignton until 11.26 am (due 10.44 am). It left at 11.30 am, as soon as the gates could be opened!

With the trains now all self-contained fixed units and only a few remaining with locomotive haulage, the operating problems are minimal compared with steam days. On 18 September 1993 HST Power Car No 43164 leads the 11.45 from Paddington over the crossing, as No 43025 waits to leave with the 15.05 to Paddington. *Both PWG*

G. W. R.

PAIGNTON

The view from the old footbridge is demonstrated in this view of BR Standard Class '7MT' 4-6-2 No 70022 *Tornado*, Newton Abbot's only 'Pacific', leaving Paignton with the up 'Devonian' in the spring of 1955. In the background can be seen Paignton's other town centre cinema, the Regent, since demolished. *The late C. H. S. Owen*

During 1993 the old up-side station buildings were demolished, revealing the old goods shed, which is now the concourse, booking office and signal box. 'Sprinter' No 150239 is having some door trouble before departing with the 13.08 service to Exmouth, hence the build-up of pedestrians waiting to cross. *PWG*

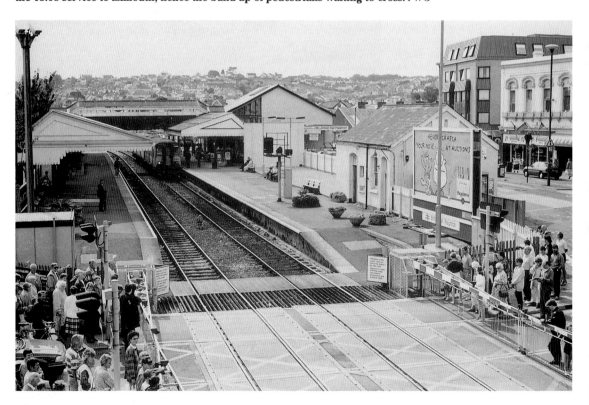

At the south end of Paignton station is the Sands Road level crossing, which would have been eliminated if Paignton had acquired its five-platform station, construction of which was stopped in 1939, never to be resumed after the war. As it was, the up platform could not be lengthened while rail access was required to the goods shed, and it has remained shorter than the down side to this day. Here 2-8-0 No 2881 is proceeding towards Torquay, with the rear of the train of tank wagons passing Paignton South Box, adjacent to the crossing, on 21 September 1951. *D. J. Frost*

Since the Paignton & Dartmouth Steam Railway acquired 'running powers' over what was previously the BR down line from Sands Road crossing to Goodrington, both BR tracks have been slewed, to become a single line over the crossing and into Goodrington Yard, using the old BR up line. A busy scene here sees 4-6-0 No 4920 *Dumbleton Hall* leaving on the 14.15 to Kingswear as Network SouthEast unit No 159011, which has arrived as the 10.12 London Waterloo to Paignton, proceeds slowly out towards Goodrington yard. Alongside the camera on 18 September 1993 HST Power Car No 43122 *South Yorkshire Metropolitan County* is about to provide rear power for the 14.30 to Newcastle. *PWG*

The view from Sands Road crossing. Like Torre and Torquay, Paignton's up platform was signalled for either-way running, and at quiet times it was and still is more convenient to use the up side. On 25 April 1952 4-6-0 No 6822 *Manton Grange* is leaving for Kingswear with the 11.40 am from Newton Abbot, a connection off the 5.30 am from Paddington. *D. J. Frost*

On summer Saturdays it is essential to use both sides and Rail Express Systems-liveried Class '47' No 47541, after arriving with the 07.45 from Liverpool, is now taking the stock out to Goodrington Yard for cleaning on 4 September 1993. The Park carriage sidings, seen on the down side in the previous picture, have now become the station and depot for the Paignton & Dartmouth Steam Railway. *PWG*

On the other side of the railway, in the days before yellow lines had been invented, an old Austin Seven stands outside the Sands Road Garage as 4-6-0 No 1010 *County of Carnarvon* (later *Caernarvon*) draws forward as far as possible with the down 'Torbay Express' on 19 August 1950, before being replaced by 4-6-0 No 6964 *Thornbridge Hall* for the remainder of the journey to Kingswear. Down trains over 13 coaches long were a severe embarrassment at Paignton, because the 14th coach obstructed the Torbay Road level crossing at the north end of the station, and as only ten coaches normally went forward to Kingswear, the crossing could be obstructed for 15 minutes or more. *D. J. Frost*

The shorter trains of 1993 present no such problem, as HST Power Car No 43028 noses its way over the Sands Road crossing with the empty set that has formed the 09.35 from Paddington on 18 September. A relay room has replaced Paignton South box and beyond the site of Sands Road Garage is the block that has replaced the Regent cinema. *PWG*

With Sands Road level crossing and Paignton South box in the background, a 'Peak' Class diesel-electric locomotive pulls out of Paignton with a summer Saturday midday arrival from the Midlands, on what was then the down line as far as Goodrington Sands Halt. The cutting was widened and this bridge replaced as part of the preparations for Paignton's new station in 1939, and the recess on the right was where the new signal box would have been built. The new station's platforms would have extended to a point level with the buffer stops on the head-shunt. *A. Hill*

By 1993 the recess has almost been covered by vegetation as 4-6-2 No 60103 *Flying Scotsman* erupts out of Paignton with the 11.35 to Kingswear on 28 August. However, the old double track line is now operated as two single lines, that on the left used only by BR, connecting the station with the carriage sidings, while the old down line is now used only by the Paignton & Dartmouth Steam Railway trains. The previous facing crossover is now reversed, and is the only link between BR and P&DSR metals. *PWG*

Looking south from the same bridge, the layout between Sands Road and Goodrington Sands Halt dated from 1930/31, when the carriage sidings and new goods shed were constructed. In this picture 4-6-0 No 6021 *King Richard II* is extracting from the yard the stock for a relief to the 4.25 pm from Paignton to Paddington on 7 June 1960, the Tuesday following the Whitsun holiday. *PWG*

By 1971 the goods shed had already been closed for six years as 'Warship' Class diesel-hydraulic No D822 *Hercules* arrives with the 16.05 Kingswear to Newton Abbot on 21 August 1971. The train in the yard is headed by sister engine No 831 *Monarch*. Both were to be withdrawn within two months. *D. H. Mitchell*

The 1993 scene is not vastly different, although the goods shed and its yard have given way to blocks of residential flats. The carriage sidings are now operated by the InterCity sector of BR and are only fully used on summer Saturdays. At about 15.30, on the last such Saturday in 1993, 2 October, Network SouthEast unit No 159015 pulls out to form the 15.46 to Southampton, leaving in the sidings, from left to right, Class '47' No D1962 (47833) *Captain Peter Manisty RN*, which had arrived on the 07.15 charter from Norwich, HST Power Car No 43044 *Borough of Kettering* with 43056 *University of Bradford* trailing, which had arrived as the 11.45 from Paddington and would be returning home as the 16.31 to Leeds, and lastly Class '47' No 47810 on the 16.11 to Liverpool. Goodrington Sands Halt can be glimpsed in the distance. *PWG*

Goodrington Sands

It is 12 November 1955 (above left) as, scooter in hand, a little boy peers through the level crossing gate at Tanners Lane, Goodrington, as 'Castle' Class 4-6-0 No 5089 *Westminster Abbey* drifts past with the down 'Torbay Express', the fireman picking up the single-line token on the other side. The abutments for the new bridge to take Tanners Road across the railway were abandoned in 1939, and work only resumed in the autumn of 1955. Being winter time the sea-front beach huts have been removed to escape the winter storms and now fill the car park. *PWG*

In the second photograph (below left), taken from the new overbridge, a few visitors are enjoying the spring sunshine in the park at Goodrington as 4-6-0 No 6814 *Enborne Grange* passes on the 3.5 pm from Exeter to Kingswear on 8 April 1960. The crew of 2-6-2T No 4105 on the up line have stopped for a word with the signalman, while in the background the goods department appears to be very busy. Very few people realised then that before the close of 1967 all goods traffic at Paignton would have ceased. *D. J. Frost*

In the third view (above) steam returns for a day to the line between Paignton and Kingswear, while a Dart Valley Railway train, brought over from Buckfastleigh, carries out some trial runs on 30 July 1972, prior to the Company purchasing the line. In the fore-ground is the Victorian saloon, with 2-6-2T No 4555 taking water from a hydrant. The signal box is still open, but since the first photo-graph was taken an additional ven-tilator has been fitted and the back window has been moved. As soon as No 4555 has been topped up, the 'Western' will move the train out past the almost deserted carriage sidings and goods shed, where the track has now been lifted, on its way back to Totnes. *PWG*

On Tuesday 21 September 1993 (right), as 4-6-0 No 4920 *Dumbleton Hall* approaches Goodrington Sands with the first train of the day at 10.33, the BR carriage sidings are empty and will remain so until the 08.15 from Leeds, the 'Devonian', runs in for servicing soon after 14.00. *PWG*

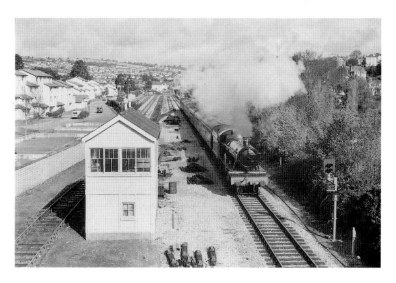

Left The only part of the pre-war planned developments at Paignton that actually matured after the war, and then not until 1955-57, were the new bridge and station at Goodrington Sands Halt, and the carriage sidings and loco-motive servicing facilities, including a new turntable, constructed alongside the station. Even as late as 1961, there were still problems finding enough siding space upon which to store all the stock arriving on the summer Saturday trains, as this picture shows. Looking south from the bridge, we see 4-6-0 No 6025 *King Henry III* pulling out the empty stock for the Sunday 4.10 pm from Paignton to Paddington on 30 July 1961. *PWG*

The situation has obviously eased by 21 August 1971, as diesel-hydraulic No D1067 *Western Druid* ticks over on the stock for the 16.20 Paignton to Kensington Olympia Motorail. The track to the steam locomotive servicing area on the right has already been lifted, but the turntable was left in situ, later to be recovered by volunteers from the Steam Railway and re-installed at Churston. *D. H. Mitchell*

Above A rare view of a 'King' Class 4-6-0 'on shed' at Goodrington. No 6002 *King William IV* takes water during the summer of 1960. *L. F. Folkard*

Below Sketch plan of Goodrington Sands station and sidings in about 1970.

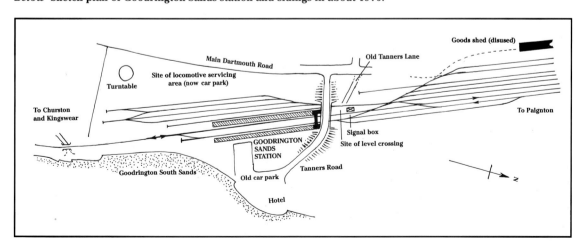

GWR 4-6-0 No 4901 *Adderley Hall* pauses at Goodrington Sands Halt in 1939, with a train for Kingswear. Opened in 1928, for that season only as Goodrington Halt, the beach facilities were then fairly basic. It was after 1936, when Paignton Urban District Council opened its new park, boating lake and children's playground, that Goodrington Sands Halt came into its own. Normally only open in those days from May to September, certain trains which would otherwise have terminated at Paignton were extended to Goodrington and then backed into the carriage sidings. The original level crossing can be glimpsed in the distance. *PWG Collection*

Since 1988 Goodrington Sands, as it is now called, has been dominated by the water slides built alongside as Stage 1 of the Quaywest complex. However, the developer collapsed before Stage 2 could be commenced and we were saved the planned three and four-storey blocks of holiday flats that were to be built between the railway and the beach. The water slides and other beach facilities have now been leased to local operators. There has been talk since 1988 of reinstating the old up line for BR services, but at present only the old down line is in use by the steam trains. One legacy of the 1988 development is a very large car park, now operated by the Borough, which makes Goodrington Sands an increasingly popular starting point for passengers on the Paignton & Dartmouth Steam Railway arriving by road.

So let's join the train for a trip down to Kingswear for Dartmouth, perhaps behind 0-6-0T No 6435, seen here standing at Goodrington Sands on 14 October 1993. *PWG*

On leaving Goodrington Sands, the line, which from here on has always been single, immediately starts to climb at a gradient of 1 in 71, steep enough to make the engine occasionally loose its grip on the rails, especially if there is a strong cross wind blowing. On Sunday 30 July 1972 the Dart Valley Light Railway Co, which at that time was running steam trains on the Buckfastleigh line, and was in negotiation with BR to purchase the Kingswear line, brought a train of its own stock across for some trial running. 2-6-2T No 4555 with three auto-trailers and the ex-GWR 'Duchess of York' saloon climbs above Goodrington South Sands, attracting the attention of the many people enjoying Sunday afternoon the beach, who have not seen a steam engine on this line for nearly ten years.

During the summer 1993 the celebrated 'Pacific' locomotive *Flying Scotsman* was visiting the Paignton & Dartmouth Steam Railway in its then new guise as BR No 60103, equipped with double chimney and smoke deflectors. The gradients were not always to this engine's liking, but on a dry rail *Scotsman* is climbing confidently above the beach, despite the on-shore breeze, with the 16.15 from Paignton on 1 September 1993. *Both PWG*

The cutting beyond Goodrington South Sands leads to this lovely red sandstone bridge taking the coastal footpath out on to the headland, while the train climbs on to a ledge above the coves of Three Beaches. 4-6-0 No 5915 *Trentham Hall* was a Reading (81D) engine, but for two months in the summer season of 1958 she was allocated to Didcot (81E), who seem to have been neglecting her maintenance. Steam leaks from every gland as she hauls the Sunday 2.20 pm from Exeter to Kingswear very slowly towards Churston on 13 July 1958.

At the same spot on 1 September 1993 2-6-2T No 4555 is having no problems with the regular seven-coach train, while across the bay the villas and hotels of Torquay bask in the warm sunshine and a 'Western Lady' ferry boat makes one of its trips around the bay. *Both PWG*

The line is forever twisting and turning, presenting fresh views for the eye to delight in, though there will not be too many people still aboard the 'Torbay Express' as it nears the end of its long journey down from London, hauled by 'Castle' Class 4-6-0 No 5053 *Earl Cairns* on 12 July 1959.

It had been very hot in 1959 when *Earl Cairns* climbed this bank, hence the almost total lack of any visible exhaust, but less so for *Flying Scotsman* in July 1973 when she made her previous visit to this line during the first summer of private operation. The engine was then in its LNER plumage as No 4472, beautifully turned out, and carrying the 'express passenger' headlamp code, one lamp over each buffer. *Both PWG*

Sugar Loaf hill, overlooking the Waterside caravan camp, with its views across to Elbury Cove and on to Brixham and Berry Head, has always been a favourite with railway photographers. On 11 September 1953 (above) Derek Frost captured one of the Newton Abbot 'Manors', No 7805 *Broome Manor*, then in plain black livery with a red-backed numberplate, though the nameplate appears black, drifting down the hill with the 3.55 pm from Kingswear to Paddington. The stock is all ex-Great Western with roof-boards reading 'PADDINGTON TORQUAY AND PAIGNTON'. The tents on the headland at this stage appear to be of the Army-surplus variety. *D. J. Frost*

On 30 July 1972 (above right) 2-6-2T No 4555 returns from Kingswear, now with the magnificent 'Duchess of York' saloon leading, the train crowded with Dart Valley Association members. A group of yachts is racing off Brixham breakwater, and the water-skiers are operating out of Elbury Cove. The headland is now alive with tents of all descriptions and a toilet block has been erected to serve them. Inland, behind the coastal footpath, mobile homes are replacing the touring caravans. *PWG*

In the third view (right), taken on 16 October 1993, the railway is having Class '50' Gala Day, organised by the Devon Diesel Society, with five engines of this Class operating all the trains, including their own engine No 50002 *Superb*, No 50042 *Triumph* from the Bodmin & Wenford Railway, and the three BR engines from Laira. Two of the Laira engines are heading this train past Waterside, No 50033 *Glorious* and No D400, on their way back to Paignton. There is now no camping on the headland, and the toilet block has been demolished. *PWG*

On a damp and dismal afternoon in late August 1960, 4-6-0 No 5992 *Horton Hall* slogs across Broadsands viaduct with the 8.5 am summer Saturday train from Cardiff to Kingswear. The land around was almost devoid of bunga-lows at that time.

The similar view on 17 October 1993 shows that hilltop now well built over, as 0-6-0T No 6435 takes the 10.30 from Paignton slowly across the viaduct; there was a 5 mph speed restriction then in force, in preparation for a major track renewal operation which was to be carried out in November. *Both PWG*

The remarkably unspoilt landscape then existing between Broadsands and Hookhills viaducts is well shown in this view taken on 27 March 1952, as the shadow of 4-6-0 No 7805 *Broome Manor* and the coaches of the 11.25 am from Cardiff to Kingswear are cast across the ploughed fields. *D. J. Frost*

As 0-6-0T No 6435 plods gingerly over the speed restricted section on 17 October 1993, it can be seen that although the acres to the seaward side of the railway are still maintained as grazing land, bungaloid growth has attacked the landward side with terminal effect. *PWG*

Also in 1952, on 24 August, 4-6-0 No 4077 *Chepstow Castle* passes the Churston fixed distant signal on the end of Hookhills viaduct. This viaduct crosses the valley leading down to the popular Broadsands beach, and is the most impressive structure on the railway. The train is the Sunday 'Torbay Express', composed mainly of post-war GWR Hawksworth designed coaches.

Today, although the fogman's hut still stands, the semaphore distant has been replaced by a colour light signal and a general increase in lineside growth hides the view obtained in 1952. Pannier tank No 6435 is pulling away from the speed restricted section with the 12.15 from Paignton on 19 October 1993. The sign in the foreground is giving a warning to trains going towards Paignton of the speed restriction that lies ahead. *Both PWG*

In summer or winter Torbay provides shelter for shipping wishing to escape rough weather in the English Channel, as this picture shows. There were evidently strong winds in the offing on Sunday 13 July 1958 as 4-6-0 No 5915 *Trentham Hall* rolled down across Hookhills viaduct with the 5.20 pm from Kingswear to Bristol, against a background of around a dozen small coasters anchored in the bay.

The 'Santa Specials' are a deservedly popular feature during December, and although, seen from the common, Hookhills viaduct now almost disappears from view during the summer behind the trees and houses that surround it, in winter it reappears to reveal 0-6-0T No 6435 as she emerges above the rooftops with Santa's train on a frosty morning in December 1991. *Both PWG*

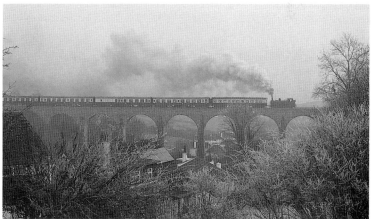

Half an hour earlier, as can be seen here, every twig had been covered in hoar frost, but the sun came out and melted it before the train arrived! *PWG*

Churston and the Brixham branch

Opposite Although Churston still displays the original 'CHURSTON FOR BRIXHAM' nameboard, sadly the journey to Brixham must now be made by road. The Brixham branch, although only two miles long, still had a substantial goods traffic in 1952, as the arrival at Churston of the branch engine, 0-4-2T No 1402, on the up goods amply demonstrates. Churston goods yard lay a little further around to the right, while the main line to Paignton dips away to the left. The long siding alongside it was used during the summer to store the stock for the Saturday 9.45 am Churston to Paddington train. *D. J. Frost*

Houses now cover the old goods yard, while the Goodrington turntable has been installed where the branch trains once ran, as 0-6-0T No 6435 completes the long climb from Goodrington to Churston with the 10.30 from Paignton on 19 October 1993. *PWG*

Above right The P&DSR's powerful 2-8-0T No 5239 *Goliath* has been out of use for several seasons, but is seen here on the turntable at Churston a few years ago. All being well, she was expected to be back in action again for 1994. *R. W. Penny*

Below Sketch map of Churston station and the junction for the Brixham branch following the closure of the latter in 1963.

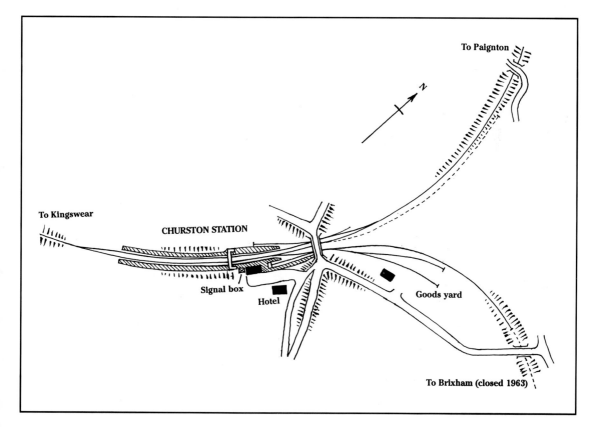

Left The two miles of the Brixham branch were relatively featureless, over comparatively level ground, terminating on a hilltop, high above the town. Consequently, at the Brixham end the line was soon built over after it closed in May 1963, while the Churston end of the line has been mainly left to nature. On 8 April 1952 the Brixham goods is approaching Churston behind 0-4-2T No 1439, having just passed the fixed distant, which can be glimpsed beyond the bridge. *D. J. Frost*

In August 1993 only the five-barred gate at the end of the field remains - just - to identify the location, the trackbed being now a jungle of vegetation. *PWG*

Above In this 1958 view of Brixham station, 0-4-2T No 1470 stands with the regular auto-trailer as a little girl talks to the engine driver. On the station the end office with the bay windows is that of the Station Master, beyond it the Waiting Room and the Ladies Room. The Gentlemen have a fine stone building at the far end, while beyond this there was an engine shed until 1929, when the branch engine was withdrawn. The site is now completely built over, and only from the Churston end does it give any impression of its previous railway use, although the road passing beneath the old station throat still carries its miles and chains from Paddington stencilled on the wall. *B. B. Williams*

Right From *Holiday Haunts*, 1937.

Back at Churston, the first picture (above), taken during the summer of 1958, shows a station more or less as it had been since the platforms were extended at the far (Kingswear) end in 1913. In 1958 it enjoyed a service of 20 down and 18 up passenger trains advertised each weekday, together with 12 return trips by the Brixham auto-train, worked on this day by 0-4-2T No 1470, which had been the regular engine on the Ashburton branch during the early 1950s. *B. B. Williams*

The late 1960s saw a complete reversal of fortune, with the Brixham branch closing in May 1963, and the sidings being taken out of use. Finally in 1968 the crossing loop was closed, and with it the signal box, which was later demolished, leaving only a single plain track through the station. This was the situation on Saturday 21 August 1971 (above right), as 'Warship' Class diesel-hydraulic No D855 *Triumph* approaches with the 08.45 from Kingswear to Cardiff, stopping to pick up returning visitors from the Brixham Holiday Camps. Mondays to Fridays a DMU was then operating a shuttle service of 12 return trips between Paignton and Kingswear. *D. H. Mitchell*

The station was in this condition or worse when the Dart Valley Light Railway Co took over at the end of 1972, and has been gradually developing ever since. The Brixham branch bay was relaid in 1976 for use by the Permanent Way Department, and the loop was restored in 1979, so that two trains could be run during the peak season. More recently the line's new workshop has been established at Churston, on the site of the old up side bay line, and brought into use during 1993, while the station building, previously let to a commercial tenant, is rapidly being refurbished by the Churston volunteers, and was again open to the public during 1993. In this view of the 'new' Churston (right), 2-6-2T No 4555 is leaving for Paignton on 2 September 1993. *PWG*

Leaving Churston, the line starts the descent towards the River Dart, passing Galmpton before diving down towards Greenway tunnel, through a tree-lined 'S'-bend, once the domain of the 'Torbay Express', headed on 9 July 1955 by 4-6-0 No 5024 *Carew Castle*.

For the peak season of 1993 it was the celebrated 'Pacific' locomotive No 60103 *Flying Scotsman* that led the trains past milepost 226 and down into the tunnel. This occasion was 2 September 1993. *Both PWG*

Greenway tunnel

Out of the deep shadow at the north end of Greenway tunnel into the strong afternoon sunlight comes 2-6-2T No 5158 with the Sunday 4.5 pm from Kingswear to Newton Abbot on 24 August 1952.

With the sun not quite so strong, 2-6-2T No 4555 emulates her larger cousin as she emerges into the daylight from this 495-yard-long tunnel on 2 September 1993. The tree growth over the tunnel mouth has been so vigorous of late that the road above is now invisible. *Both PWG*

Although cutting back of the lineside vegetation is still carried out on a regular basis, it is not done either so often, nor as assiduously as it was years ago, in the days of the lengthman and his gang. The Kingswear end of Greenway tunnel in 1960 displays the superbly tidy appearance of a well-trimmed lawn, as BR Class '9F' 2-10-0 No 92216 coasts down towards Kingswear with the 9.05 am from Swansea on Saturday 27 August.

It is still cared for, but not quite so tidy in 1993, as 4-6-0 No 4920 *Dumbleton Hall* potters down the gradient with the 16.15 from Paignton on 28 September. *Both PWG*

Once out of the tunnel the line swings across Maypool viaduct and down through Long Wood towards the ship-yards at Noss, with the River Dart getting ever closer on the right. On 27 August 1960 we see 4-6-0 No 5992 *Horton Hall* climbing towards the tunnel across the viaduct with the Saturday 3.20 pm from Kingswear to Cardiff.

Despite the violent storms of recent years, which have felled a few of the weaker specimens, most of the trees continue to grow larger, year by year, especially on these sheltered southern slopes. The view of the river has now almost disappeared, though *Dumbleton Hall* can be seen and heard as she pulls across the viaduct with the last train of the day on 28 September 1993. *Both PWG*

Britannia Halt

Britannia Halt, or Kingswear Crossing as it was officially known, was an unadvertised stopping place originally constructed in 1877 for the Prince of Wales, who was bringing his two sons to join HMS Britannia as naval cadets. In later years it seems mainly to have been used by workers at the Philip & Sons shipyard at Noss, for whom a morning down train and an evening up one were stopped here, with a lunchtime return service on Saturdays. Its best service was during the war, when three trains a day each way stopped here. *D. H. Mitchell*

When the first picture was taken in 1971, the Steam Ferry Crossing Ground Frame controlled only the level crossing gates and the approach signals, but by 1993 this box now controls not only the lifting barriers installed during the winter of 1987-8, but also the points and signals for the whole line between Paignton and Kingswear. Sadly, Britannia Halt is no more, having been demolished during that same winter of 1987-8. *PWG*

With its fourth coach abreast of Britannia Halt, and Kingswear station in the distance, the 8.45 am from Kingswear to Bradford (Forster Square), the 'Devonian', commences the climb to Churston behind 4-6-0 No 5053 *Earl Cairns* in July 1959. Also in view is the old 1896 steam ferry, operating the Floating Bridge or Higher Ferry, which was due to be replaced by the present ferry in 1960. *D. S. Fish*

With the Higher Ferry vessel away on the Dartmouth side, 0-6-0T No 6435 operates a short demonstration train of PW Dept wagons past the site of Britannia Halt on 21 June 1992. *R. W. Penny*

Seen from the slipway of the Higher Ferry, soon after leaving Kingswear, are 4-4-0 No 3440 *City of Truro* and 2-6-2T No 4179, with a returning Swindon to Kingswear excursion on 19 May 1957. Against the dark waters of the River Dart, the effect in colour was quite striking, with *City of Truro* in Great Western lined green and the tank in clean BR black, and the coaches in red and cream with a maroon kitchen car. *L. F. Folkard*

The Inaugural Day for the private Paignton & Dartmouth Steam Railway was on 31 December 1972, when 2-6-2T No 4588 worked the trains with bunting wrapped around her smokebox handrails. The trains consisted of three BR-built Great Western-style auto-trailers brought over from Buckfastleigh. *PWG*

Kingswear

Just in case anyone should think that tender-first running is a feature only of preserved lines with no turning facilities at either end of the line, this picture of 4-6-0 No 5059 *Earl St Aldwyn* piloting 2-6-2T No 4117 out of Kingswear with the 4.33 pm to Exeter on 18 May 1957 should disillusion them. The 'Castle' will be leaving this train at Goodrington, to pick up a goods train from the yard, which it will then work to Newton Abbot.

On 23 September 1993 4-6-0 No 4920 *Dumbleton Hall* leaves Kingswear for Paignton on the 17.00 service, with the 'Devon Belle' observation saloon next to the engine. Note the 'banjo' bus-turning circle on the road above the station, built over the site of the GWR water tank. *Both PWG*

Left Holiday Runabout Ticket advertisement from the summer of 1959.

Opposite On 16 April 1956 4-6-0 No 4082 *Windsor Castle* (alias No 7013 *Bristol Castle*) rolls in over Hoodown crossing with the 'Torbay Express' almost at the end of its run down from Paddington. From the hillside above, a wartime pillbox looks down menacingly. *B. B. Williams*

The pillbox is now suitably cloaked in shrubbery, but its corner can still be seen, as 4-6-0 No 4920 *Dumbleton Hall* passes the steel replacement for the earlier GWR wooden post semaphore, now carrying only colour light signals, with the 16.15 from Paignton on 23 September 1993. Hoodown viaduct, in the foreground, was a double-track replacement in 1928 for an earlier single-line wooden structure that had prevented the heavier GWR engines from entering Kingswear. In 1924 the working timetable indicated that the 'Torbay Express' changed engines at Torquay in both directions, because of this restriction. *PWG*

Below Sketch map of the terminus at Kingswear in the 1950s.

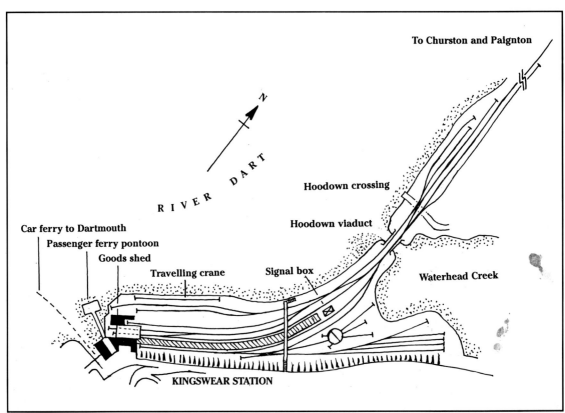

To Churston and Paignton

N

RIVER DART

Hoodown crossing

Hoodown viaduct

Car ferry to Dartmouth
Passenger ferry pontoon
Goods shed
Travelling crane
Signal box
Waterhead Creek

KINGSWEAR STATION

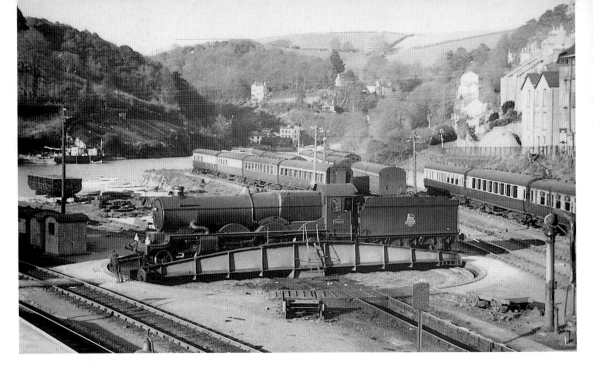

While the Hoodown viaduct was being rebuilt, the opportunity was taken to replace the existing turntable with a new 65-foot model to take the largest engines. 'Castle' Class 4-6-0 No 7000 *Viscount Portal* is seen in the first view being turned by hand on this table on 21 April 1951. *The late C. H. S. Owen*

The area previously used for the turntable pit and carriage sidings is now the car park at Kingswear, adjacent to the new Marina level crossing, seen on 19 October 1993. *PWG*

The derelict air surrounding the whole railway as BR left it at the end of 1972 is well shown in this view of ex-LNER 4-6-2 No 4472 *Flying Scotsman* approaching the platform end at Kingswear during the railway's first season as a private operation in July 1973.

On a very misty Gala Day, 30 August 1993 (it cleared up later), 2-6-2Ts Nos 4588 and 4555 double-head down from Paignton on one of the morning trains. If the present scene at Kingswear is not to everyone's liking, at least it does look far more productive than it did in 1973. *Both PWG*

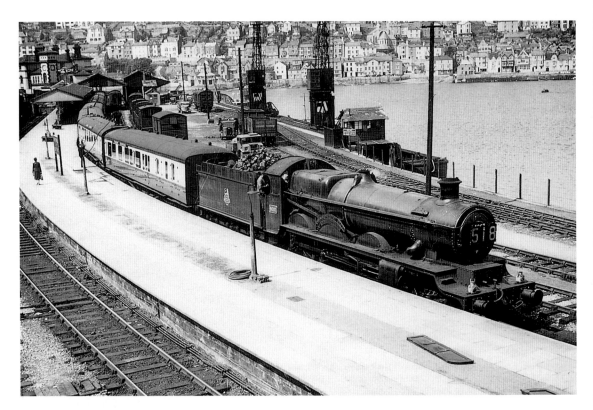

Standing in Kingswear station in fine fettle, at the head of the prestige express train, the 'Torbay Express', 'Star' Class 4-6-0 No 4007 *Swallowfield Park* (above left) does not look like an engine that is about to be withdrawn from service at the end of the season. But it was, in September 1951. In the background is a busy Kingswear goods yard, with some interesting road vehicles being loaded from the railway wagons. There is no collier at the quayside, so the GWR's electric cranes, installed for the coal traffic in 1932, are at rest. *PWG Collection*

An entirely different scene presents itself in the second view 20 years later, on 18 September 1971 (left), as the DMU shuttle (Nos 51095, 59426 and 51067) leaves for Paignton. Only the one platform line and the run-round loop remain. The black goods shed still stands, but the goods yard is now a car park, with the old roofed ferry pontoon visible beyond. The three-masted sailing ship may be one of those used during the filming of TV's *The Onedin Line*, where Bayard's Cove at Dartmouth was cast as Liverpool. *D. H. Mitchell*

Today's scene (above) is far more lively, if not entirely typical, with Network SouthEast Class '159' unit No 159003 *Templecombe* in the bay platform, as *Dumbleton Hall* pulls forward in the distance to run around the regular train. Fish lorries load at the quayside, where the old goods shed has been demolished, and the Devon Diesel Society's Class '50', No 50002 *Superb*, rests on the loop headshunt. The Class '159' unit was on a special charter outing from Waterloo, in the course of which it had been officially named *Templecombe* during a short stop there that morning 3 October 1993. It is seen awaiting the return of its passengers from a river trip. *PWG*

The interior of Kingswear station also had a woebegone appearance on 18 September 1971, as DMU Nos 51067, 59426 and 51095 stands on arrival with the 7.10 am service from Paignton. *D. H. Mitchell*

On 19 October 1993 0-6-0T No 6435 is running around the train prior to returning with the 13.00 service to Paignton. The station now looks in far better shape, even if the view of it is partially obstructed by the white paling fence, reflecting the many hours of work put into it by the small band of volunteers responsible for the station. *PWG*

To Dartmouth

Since the whole object of the railway was to reach and serve the town of Dartmouth, and the railway provided a station on each side of the river, it was also necessary to provide a ferry service to connect the two stations. During the 19th century the ferry rights were leased out, but from 1901 the GWR ran the ferry itself, at first with the *Dolphin*, a 61-ton iron paddler, but she was replaced by the well-loved *The Mew* in 1908, which continued to serve the town until 1954. *The Mew* is seen here approaching the Kingswear pontoon on 4 September 1954, one month before she was withdrawn from service.

During the summer of 1993, the passenger ferry service was operated by several boats, but the one most often meeting the trains was the *Kingswear Belle*, seen leaving Kingswear on 10 September 1993. *Both PWG*

This postcard view of the embankment at Dartmouth was taken before 1908, while the *Dolphin* was still in service, from a very new-looking pontoon, with the GWR's famous 'station without trains' beyond. *PWG Collection*

In recent years the embankment has been still further extended into the river, the old GWR station is now the Station Restaurant, and the new pontoon, at which the *Kingswear Belle* and several other vessels are moored, has no roof. On the far side of the river, *Dumbleton Hall* is commencing the climb away from the river bank, beyond the Higher Ferry slipway, with the 15.15 service from Kingswear. *PWG*

The change in the nature and quantity of the river traffic over the past 60 years can be gauged from these final two pictures, the first taken in the 1930s, when many commercial steamers were laid up in the river above the Higher Ferry during the Slump, and paddle steamers ran the river service between Dartmouth and Totnes. *PWG Collection*

The second was taken on 19 October 1993 as 0-6-0T No 6435 approaches the new level crossing over the railway into the Marina at Kingswear, and shows the vast increase in small pleasure craft now moored in the river. *PWG*

Timetables: 1934, 1954, 1971/2 and 1973/4

GWR local timetable, Summer 1934

NEWTON ABBOT, TORQUAY AND DARTMOUTH.

WEEK-DAYS.

(Side banner: SIMONDS LUNCHEON STOUT)

Stations listed: NEWTON ABBOT dep., Kingskerswell, Torre arr., TORQUAY { arr. / dep. }, Paignton, Goodrington Sands Ht., Churston, Kingswear arr., DARTMOUTH.

A Mondays only (August Bank Holiday excepted).   G Saturdays excepted.   J Saturdays only, and will not run after September 15th.   P Runs Saturdays and also on Friday, August 3rd.   Q 10 minutes later on Saturdays.   R Paignton arrive 4.55 p.m. (5.8 p.m. on Saturdays).   S Saturdays only.
T Through Train from Paddington, depart 12.0 noon.   ‡ Paignton arrive 6.51 p.m.

NEWTON ABBOT, TORQUAY AND DARTMOUTH.

SUNDAYS.

(Side banner: SIMONDS "HOP" LEAF PRODUCTS)

Stations listed: NEWTON ABBOT dep., Kingskerswell, Torre arr., TORQUAY { arr. / dep. }, Paignton, Goodrington Sands Ht., Churston, Kingswear arr., DARTMOUTH.

CHEAP RETURN TICKETS TO CORNWALL.

CHEAP DAY TICKETS (First and Third Class) at approximately the single fare for the double journey will be issued from Exeter and all G.W. Stations West thereof to Any G.W. Station in Cornwall where the Forward and Return Journeys can be made the same day.
Intending Passengers should enquire at the Stations for train times and fares.

DARTMOUTH, TORQUAY AND NEWTON ABBOT.

WEEK-DAYS.

(Timetable — a.m. and p.m. columns for stations: Dartmouth dep., Kingswear, Churston, Goodrington Sands Halt, Paignton, Torquay arr./dep., Torre, Kingskerswell, Newton Abbot arr.)

B Mondays only (August Bank Holiday excepted); will also run on Tuesday, August 7th. E Fridays and Saturdays only. F Fridays only.
G Saturdays excepted. J Saturdays only and will not run after September 15th. K Paignton arrive 12.26 p.m. S Saturdays only. V Through
Train to Paddington, arrive 3.35 p.m. (Saturdays 8.50 p.m.). X Saturdays only. Through Train to South Wales.

DARTMOUTH, TORQUAY AND NEWTON ABBOT.—continued.

SUNDAYS.

(Timetable — a.m. and p.m. columns for stations: Dartmouth dep., Kingswear, Churston, Goodrington Sands Halt, Paignton, Torquay arr./dep., Torre, Kingskerswell, Newton Abbot arr.)

HALF-DAY EXCURSIONS,

TUESDAYS, WEDNESDAYS & THURSDAYS, (FROM JULY 10th TO SEPTEMBER 27th, 1934, INCLUSIVE.)

TO
TORQUAY and PAIGNTON

Return Fare **2/6** Third Class.

EXETER (St. David's) dep. 12.40, 1.20, or 2.19 p.m.
EXETER (St. Thomas) dep. 12.45, 1.24, or 2.24 p.m.
Passengers may Return by any Train on the Day of Outward Journey.

Return Fare **2/6** Third Class.

Great Western Railway.
THIRD CLASS
Holiday Season Ticket.
(1 week)
No. 206
District 4. Rate 10/-
M. WOOD
From 17 AUG to
23 AUG 1935
AVAILABLE BETWEEN
PLYMOUTH, Millbay,
ST. BUDEAUX PLATFORM,
KINGSBRIDGE, ASHBURTON,
KINGSWEAR, DARTMOUTH,
BRIXHAM and
DAWLISH WARREN
And all Intermediate Stations
This Ticket to be given up on expiry
(Dartmouth).

Table 89

BR timetable, Summer 1954

Table 89

Table 89 — NEWTON ABBOT, TORQUAY, PAIGNTON and DARTMOUTH

Mondays to Fridays

TORBAY EXPRESS

THE DEVONIAN

Saturdays

Sundays

Stations (reading down):
6 London (Pad.) ... dep
6 Liverpool (L.St.) ... "
6 Manchester (L.Rd) ... "
6 Birmingham (General) ... "
6 Cardiff (General) ... "
6 Bristol (T.Mds.) ... "
Newton Abbot ... dep
Kingskerswell ... "
Torre ... "
8 Torquay ... { arr / dep }
8 Paignton ... "
8 Goodrington Sands Halt ... "
11 Churston (for Brixham) ... "
14½ Kingswear ... arr
Dartmouth ¶ ... arr

Reference notes:
A Through Train between Saltash and Goodrington Sands Halt
a a.m.
B Applies 28th June to 21st August inclusive
b Includes Refreshment/Car Train
c Applies 10th July to 28th August inclusive
D Runs 10th July to 14th August
E Friday nights only
H Runs 3rd July to 14th August
J On Sunday nights dep. Liverpool (Lime St.) 5 25 p.m. and Manchester (London Rd.) 5 30 p.m. (via Birmingham (New St.) and Cardiff (General))
J Friday nights and will not run inclusive 3rd June to 28th August and after 3rd September
K Runs 3rd July to 21st August inclusive
L Dep. 3 15 p.m. on Fridays Runs 23rd July to 7th August inclusive
M Birmingham (Victoria) via Hereford Friday nights only
P Runs on 19th June, 4th, 11th and 18th September only
V Arr. Paignton 6 22 a.m. and Churston 5 45 a.m.
W Manchester (Victoria) via Cheltenham Spa (Lansdown). Runs 12th July to 3rd September
X Friday nights and applies 2nd July to 27th August inclusive
Y Will not run after 11th September
Z Through Train to or from Bovey and Moretonhampstead
§ Through Carriages to Kingswear
§ Third class only
† Will not run after 4th September
‡ Dep. 7 45 a.m. from 24th July to 7th August inclusive
◇ Arr. 4 25 a.m.
□ By Steamer

RC — Restaurant Car
SC — First and Third Class Sleeping Cars

Table 89 — NEWTON ABBOT, TORQUAY, PAIGNTON and DARTMOUTH

Table 89

Table 89 — continued

Saturdays — continued

TORBAY EXPRESS

Sundays

THE DEVONIAN

Sundays — continued

TORBAY EXPRESS

Stations (reading down):
6 London (Pad.) ... dep
6 Liverpool (L.St.) ... "
6 Manchester (L.Rd) ... "
6 Birmingham (General) ... "
6 Cardiff (General) ... "
6 Bristol (T.Mds.) ... "
Newton Abbot ... dep
Kingskerswell ... "
Torre ... "
Torquay ... { arr / dep }
Paignton ... "
Goodrington Sands Halt ... "
Churston (for Brixham) ... "
Kingswear ... arr
Dartmouth ¶ ... arr

Reference notes:
A Through Train between Saltash and Goodrington Sands Halt
Δ Change at Newport
B Runs 3rd July to 28th August inclusive
C Applies 6th July to 28th August inclusive
E Through Carriages to Kingswear
F Bristol (Stapleton Road). Through Carriages from Newton Abbot
G Saturdays 26th June only
H Runs 26th June, 3rd, 8th, 15th, 22nd and 29th August only
K Birmingham (New St.) via Cheltenham Spa (Lansdown)
X Will not run after 28th August inclusive
P Refreshment Car, in some cases for a portion of the journey only
SC First and Third class Sleeping Cars (limited accommodation)
I Through Carriages to Paignton or ◇ § will not run after 4th September
J Birmingham (Moor St.)
X Through Carriages from Bristol to Paignton and Goodrington Sands Halt
y Runs 3rd July to 4th September inclusive
Z Through Train to or from Bovey and Moretonhampstead
§ Through Carriages to Kingswear
† By Steamer
‡ Via Birmingham (New St.) and Cheltenham Spa (Lansdown)

Table 89

Table 89—continued DARTMOUTH, PAIGNTON, TORQUAY and NEWTON ABBOT

Mondays to Fridays

Saturdays

Mondays to Fridays—continued

Saturdays—continued

Stations (with Miles):

Miles	Station
—	Dartmouth ¶ ...... dep
—	Kingswear
3½	Churston (for Brixham)
6	Goodrington Sands Halt
6½	Paignton
9½	Torquay ...... {arr / dep}
12½	Torre ...... {dep / arr}
12½	Kingskerswell
14½	Newton Abbot ...... arr
18½	Bristol (T. Mds.) ...... arr
122½	Cardiff (General) ...... arr
188½	Birmingham (S.H.) ...... arr
231½	Manchester (L.Rd.) ...... arr
248½	Liverpool (L. St.) ...... arr
228½	London (Pad.) ...... arr

THE DEVONIAN

TORQUAY EXPRESS

Table 89—continued DARTMOUTH, PAIGNTON, TORQUAY and NEWTON ABBOT

Saturdays

Sundays

Saturdays—continued

Sundays—continued

TORQUAY EXPRESS

Notes (footnote legends)

A Runs 10th July to 4th Sept. incl.
a.m.
B Through Train to Sheffield. From 16th July to 29th August inclusive extended to Leeds. Arrives 4 13 p.m.
C Through Train to Cardiff (General)
D Runs 3rd July to 11th Sept. incl.
E Through Train to Cardiff (General)
F Through Train to Bradford (F. Sq.)

(additional small-type note about Reserved Seat tickets / passengers travelling by this train)

G Friday nights only
H Through Train to Plymouth
J Through Train to Birmingham (Snow Hill) and Wolverhampton (Low Level)
K From 26th June to 28th July, incl.
L Through Carriages from Bovey and Moretonhampstead
m Through Train to Manchester
n Commences 3rd July. Through Train to Newcastle
o Through Train to Nottingham
p Through Carriages from Goodrington Sands Halt, via Cheltenham Spa (Lansdown), Arr. 3 26 p.m.

P Thursdays only
Q Refreshment Car on Mondays
R Refreshment Car
RC Refreshment Car
S Runs 19th and 26th June only
† Refreshment Car
T Through Carriages from Kingswear
U Third class only
† Arr. 2 20 p.m. on 4th, 11th and 18th September
Through Carriages from Kingswear
Arr. 6 50 p.m. on Fridays
¶ By Steamer

(Right-hand column notes, second table:)

h Through Train to Birmingham and Wolverhampton
j For service to London until 4th Sept., see next column but one. September only
J Through Train to Cardiff (Gen.)
L Through Carriages from Bovey and Moretonhampstead
m Through Train to (or from) Bovey and Moretonhampstead
M Through Train to Manchester
n Through Train to Newcastle
o Through Train to Nottingham
H Passengers travelling in First and Third class Sleeping Cars (limited accommodation) from Newton Abbot after 6 15 a.m.
Through Train to London (Pad.)
V Manchester (Vic.) via Hereford
W Runs 12th July to 3rd September inclusive
X Through Train to London (Pad.)
Y Will not run after 11th September
Z Through Train to Manchester

RC or R Refreshment Car. In some cases for a portion of the journey only
SC First and Third class Sleeping Cars (limited accommodation). Newton Abbot to London (Pad.)
T Through Carriage from Paignton
U Runs 24th June to 3rd July
   Arr. 3 18 p.m. from Newton Abbot, 4th September
* Birmingham (Moor Street)
V Runs 31st July to 28th August
W Will not run 31st July to 29th inclusive
X Refreshment Car provided 26th June to 21st August inclusive
Y Through Train to London (Pad.)
Z Runs 18th July to 29th Aug. incl.
p.m. Through Train 18th July to 14th Aug. incl.
Through Carriage from Kingswear
By Steamer
Applies 4th July to 12th Sept. incl.

Table 28

Paignton, Kingswear and Dartmouth (Second class only unless otherwise shown)

Mondays to Fridays also Saturdays
from 2 October

Miles			A				SO	SX										
0	PAIGNTON	d	05 25	..	07 42	..	08 40	..	09 45 10 35 10 40	..	12 15	..	13 30	..	14 15	..	15 50	..	17 19	..	18 01	..	18 55
	GOODRINGTON SANDS	d	..	..	..	..	..	..	09b48 .. 10b43	..	..	..	13b33	..	14b18	..	15b53	..	17b22	..	18b04	..	18b58
3	CHURSTON (FOR BRIXHAM Z)	d	05 42	..	07 51	..	08 49	..	09 55 10 45 10 50	..	12 25	..	13 40	..	14 25	..	16 00	..	17 29	..	18 11	..	19 05
6½	KINGSWEAR	a	05 50	..	07 59	..	08 59	..	10 03 10 53 10 58	..	12 33	..	13 48	..	14 33	..	16 08	..	17 37	..	18 19	..	19 13
7	†DARTMOUTH (FOR KINGSBRIDGE)	a	06 24	..	08 09	..	09 09	..	10 24 11 09 11 09	..	12 54	..	14 09	..	14 54	..	16 24	..	17 54	..	18 39	..	19 24

Saturdays
Until 25 September

					C		B					D							
PAIGNTON	..	d	05 25	..	07 10 08 11	..	09 15	..	09 58	..	10 55	..	12 25	..	13 15	..	14 35	..	15 25 16 23 17 25	..	18 15 19 35	..
GOODRINGTON SANDS	..	d	..	..	..	..	..	..	..	..	10 58	..	12b28	..	13b18	..	14b38	..	16e26 17e28	..	18e18 19e38	..
CHURSTON (FOR BRIXHAM Z)	..	d	05 42	..	07 19 08 20	..	09 24	..	10 07	..	11 05	..	12 43	..	13 25	..	14 53	..	15 37 16 33 17 43	..	18 33 19 45	..
KINGSWEAR	..	a	05 50	..	07 27 08 30	..	09 32	..	10 15	..	11 13	..	12 43	..	13 33	..	14 53	..	15 45 16 41 17 43	..	18 33 19 45	..
†DARTMOUTH (FOR KINGSBRIDGE)	..	a	06 24	..	07 39 08 39	..	10 09	..	10 39	..	11 24	..	12 54	..	13 54	..	15 09	..	16 09 16 54 17 54	..	18 54 20 09	..

Dartmouth, Kingswear and Paignton (Second class only unless otherwise shown)

Mondays to Fridays also Saturdays
from 2 October

Miles					A SO SX												
0	†DARTMOUTH (FOR KINGSBRIDGE)	d	06 30	..	08 00	..	09 00 10 00	..	10 45 11 15	..	12 45 13 30	..	14 30	..	16 00	..	17 30	..	18 00	..	19 15
½	KINGSWEAR	d	06 43	..	08 11	..	09 19 10 10	..	11 00 11 25	..	13 05 13 52	..	14 45	..	16 15	..	17 40	..	18 22	..	19 30
4	CHURSTON (FOR BRIXHAM Z)	d	06 52	..	08 20	..	09 28 10 19	..	11 09 11 34	..	13 36	..	14 54	..	16 24	..	17 50	..	18 31	..	19 39
6½	GOODRINGTON SANDS	d	..	..	..	..	09b33 10b24	..	11b39	..	13b19 14b06	..	14b59	..	16b29	..	17b55	..	18b36	..	19b44
7	PAIGNTON	a	07 00	..	08 28	..	09 36 10 27	..	11 17 11 42	..	13 22 14 09	..	15 02	..	16 32	..	17 58	..	18 39	..	19 47

Saturdays
Until 25 September

			◆		◆	J b		D ●		◆		◆		◆		A			
†DARTMOUTH (FOR KINGSBRIDGE)	d	06 30	..	07 15 08 30	..	09 15	..	10 15	..	11 15	..	12 30	..	13 15	..	14 45	..	15 45 16 45 17 30	..	18 30 19 45	..
KINGSWEAR	d	06 43	..	07 31 08 45	..	09 35	..	10 30	..	11 27	..	12 47	..	13 36	..	15 05	..	16 05 17 00 17 47	..	18 40 20 00	..
CHURSTON (FOR BRIXHAM Z)	d	06 59	..	07 40 08 54	..	09 45	..	10 43	..	11 37	..	12 57	..	13 46	..	15 15	..	16 14 17 09 17 47	..	18 50 20 00	..
GOODRINGTON SANDS	d	..	..	..	..	..	..	..	..	11e43	..	13e03	..	13e52	..	15e21	..	17e16 18e03	..	18e56 20e16	..
PAIGNTON	a	07 06	..	07 47 09 02	..	09 52	..	10 51	..	11 45	..	13 05	..	13 54	..	15 23	..	16 22 17 18 18 05	..	18 58 20 18	..

Heavy figures denote through carriages;
light figures denote connecting services
For general notes see pages 4 and 5

A From or to Newton Abbot (Table 3)
B ⬛ from Newton Abbot (Table 3)
C From 12 June is ⬛ from Newton Abbot (Table 1)
D ⬛ from or to London Paddington (Table 3)
J From 12 June is ⬛ to Cardiff General (Table 3)
Z A frequent service of Devon General Buses operates
between Paignton Bus Station (adjacent to Railway
Station), Churston Railway Station Approach Road
(200 yards from Station) and Brixham. See pages
10 to 18

b Mondays to Fridays 7 June to 3 September
● 12 June to 4 September
† By BR Ferry from Kingswear.
See pages 10 to 18 for bus service to Kingsbridge

■ **WEST COUNTRY HOLIDAY TRAIN**
From 12 June passengers travelling to South Wales
must book seats. See pages 29 and 30.

● **WEST COUNTRY HOLIDAY TRAIN**
From 5 June passengers travelling to Reading or
Paddington must book seats. See page 28.

◆ Passengers travelling by this service to connect
into West Country Holiday trains to certain destinations must book seats. See Table 3 and
pages 28 to 30.

| Table 35a | | **Torbay Steam Railway — Paignton and Kingswear** | | | | | | | | | | | | | | |

DAILY UNTIL 7 OCTOBER

			SSuX	SSuX								A	B	B			
PAIGNTON	..	d	07 28	08 45	..	10 02	11 23	..	12 44	..	14 05	..	15 36	..	17 40	..	19(30	..	20(47	..	22(02	..
GOODRINGTON SANDS	..	d	..	..	..	10 06	11 27	..	12 48	..	14 19	..	15 40	..	17 44	..	..	..	..	..
CHURSTON (FOR BRIXHAM Z)	..	d	07 42	08 59	..	10 18	11 39	..	13 00	..	14 31	..	15 52	..	17 56	..	19(44	..	21(01	..	22(16	..
KINGSWEAR (FOR DARTMOUTH†)	a	..	07 45	09 12	..	10 31	11 52	..	13 13	..	14 44	..	16 05	..	18 09	..	19(57	..	21(14	..	22(29	..

			SSuX	SSuX							A	B	C	D			
KINGSWEAR (FOR DARTMOUTH†)	d	08 05	09 22	..	10 41	12 02	..	13 23	14 54	..	16 15	..	18 19	..	20(07	..	21(24	..	22(45	..	23(20	..
CHURSTON (FOR BRIXHAM Z)	..	d	08 20	09 37	..	10 56	12 17	..	13 38	15 09	..	16 30	..	18 34	..	20(22	..	21(39	..	23(00	..	23(35	..
GOODRINGTON SANDS	..	d	..	..	..	11 06	12 27	..	13 48	15 19	..	16 40	..	18 44	..	..	..	..	..
PAIGNTON	..	a	08 33	09 50	..	11 12	12 32	..	13 53	15 24	..	16 45	..	18 49	..	20(35	..	21(52	..	23(13	..	23(48	..

† By ER ferry from Kingswear

For service from 8 October see
subsequent announcement

A 27 May to 22 September
B 9 July to 22 September
C 9 July to 28 August and 2 to 22 September
D 29 August to 1 September
Z A frequent service of Devon General buses operates
between Paignton Bus Station (adjacent to Railway
Station), Churston Railway Station Approach Road
(200 yards from Station) and Brixham.

BR timetable, 1971-2, the last year of BR operation of the line

BR timetable for 1973-4, showing the first season of private operation of the line